Rape: A Bibliography
1965-1975

Rape: A Bibliography

1965-1975

Compiled by

Dorothy L. Barnes

The Whitston Publishing Company

Troy, New York

1977

PREFACE

Rape, a Bibliography, 1965-1975 is a virtually comprehensive list of books and journal articles that will satisfy the needs of all but the most specialized searcher. Thirty one indexes, abstracts, catalogs and bibliographies from many different disciplines were consulted. All aspects of rape have been included, from medical to legal to feminist concerns.

The problem of rape has been widely discussed in recent years, and this bibliography is intended to provide easy access to its literature. It is surprising, however, that so little has been written about rape. The majority of the material listed here appeared in the 1970's. But within the past five years there has been no significant increase in publication concerning the subject; rather a stabilization or slight decline.

The following titles were the major sources: *Alternative Press Index, American Reference Books Annual, Bibliographic Index, Books in Print, British Humanities Index, Business Periodicals Index, Canadian Periodical Index, Crime & Delinquency Literature, Cumulative Book Index, Cumulated Index to Nursing Literature, Dissertation Abstracts International—Humanities and Social Sciences, Education Index, Hospital Literature Index, Humanities Index, Index Medicus, Index to Legal Periodicals, Index to Periodical Articles Related to Law, International Bibliography of the Social Sciences, International Nursing Index, Library of Congress Catalog—Books: Subjects, Philosophers Index, Psychological Abstracts, Public Affairs Information Service (PAIS), Public Affairs Information Service Foreign Language Index, Readers' Guide to Periodical Literature, Research in Education, Social Sciences and Humanities Index, Social Sciences Index, Social Sciences Citation Index, Sociological Abstracts, Women*

Studies Abstracts. All were searched from 1965 through 1975, or in some cases June 1976. A few citations taken from various essays and books have also been included.

The bibliography is arranged in four sections. Books are listed alphabetically by author. Journal articles are listed alphabetically by article title. A subject section is provided for the journal articles. The 126 subject terms used in the subject analysis have been generated by the material itself. A list of these subject heads follows this preface. Because of the non-descriptive titles of some of the journal articles, a few have been omitted from the subject section. The final section is the author index to the journal articles. Alphabetization throughout the bibliography is letter-by-letter. Punctuation and capitalization are ignored.

Care has been taken to standardize the citation format. Although not all citations include identical elements (i.e., some include issue numbers while others use only dates), they are adequate to locate the material.

Journal abbreviations are in many cases unique to this volume; a list of the journal abbreviations used follows the preface.

LIST OF PERIODICAL ABBREVIATIONS

ABA J	American Bar Association Journal
ABST ON CRIM & PENOL	Abstracts on Criminology and Penology
ACTA MED LEG SOC	ACTA Medicinae Legalis Et Socialis (Liege)
ACTA PSYCHIAT SCAND SUPPL	ACTA Psychiatrica Scandinavica Supplement
ADVOCATE	Advocate
AIN'T I A WOMAN	Ain't I a Woman?
AKRON L REV	Akron Law Review
AKUSH GINEK	Akusherstvo i Ginekologiia; Supplement to Suvremenna Meditsina (Sofiia)
ALA L REV	Alabama Law Review
ALBANY LAW R	Albany Law Review
AM CRIM L Q	American Criminal Law Quarterly
AM CRIM L REV	American Criminal Law Review
AM DRUGGIST	American Druggist
AM J CRIM L	American Journal of Criminal Law
AM J NURSING	American Journal of Nursing
AM J OBSTET GYNECOL	American Journal of Obstetrics and Gynecology
AM J ORTHOP	American Journal of Orthopsychiatry
AM J PSYCH	American Journal of Psychiatry
AM J SOC	American Journal of Sociology
AM MED NEWS	American Medical News (American Medical Association)
AM POETRY REV	American Poetry Review
ANN AM ACAD POLITIC & SOC SCI	American Academy of Political and Social Science. Annals
ANN ARBOR SUN	Ann Arbor Sun
ANN INTERN MED	Annals of Internal Medicine
ANN NY ACAD SCI	Annals of the New York Academy of Sciences
APHRA	Aphra

ARCH KRIMINOL	Archiv fur Kriminologie (Lubeck)
ARCH OF SEX BEH	Archives of Sexual Behavior
ARIZ L REV	Arizona Law Review
ARIZ MED	Arizona Medicine
ATLANTIC MONTH	Atlantic Monthly
AUGUR	Augur
AUST J POL	Australian Journal of Politics and History
AUSTRALAS NURSES J	Australian Nurses' Journal
AUSTRALIAN & NEW ZEALAND J OF CRIM	Australian and New Zealand Journal of Criminology
BAYLOR L REV	Baylor Law Review
BEH RES & THER	Behaviour Research and Therapy
BEH THER	Behavior Therapy
BERKELEY TRIBE	Berkeley Tribe
BIRTH FAM J	Birth and the Family Journal
BLACK PANTH	Black Panther
BLACK SCHOLAR	Black Scholar
BRIT J ADDICT	British Journal of Addiction
BRIT J CRIM	British Journal of Criminology
BRIT MED J	British Medical Journal
BROADSHEET: NEW ZEALAND'S FEM MAG	Broadsheet: New Zealand's Feminist Magazine
BROOK BARR	Brooklyn Barrister
BROOK L REV	Brooklyn Law Review
BROTHER	Brother
BULL AM COLL SURG	American College of Surgeons. Bulletin
BULL AM PROTE HOSP ASS	American Protestant Hospital Association. Bulletin
CAL J	California Journal
CALIF L REV	California Law Review
CAN FORUM	Canadian Forum
CAN MENT HEALTH	Canada's Mental Health/Hygiene
CAN NURSE	Canadian Nurse
CASE AND COM	Case and Comment
CATHOLIC U L REV	Catholic University Law Review
CESK GYNEKOL	Ceskoslovenska Gynekologie (Praha)
CHATELAINE	Chatelaine
CHILD PSYCH AND HUM DEV	Child Psychiatry and Human Development

CHR TODAY	Christianity Today
CLEV ST L R	Cleveland State Law Review
CLIN PEDIAT	Clinical Pediatrics
COLD DAY IN AUGUST	Cold Day in August
COLL PRESS SER	College Press Service
COLUM L REV	Columbia Law Review
COMMONWEAL	Commonweal
CONN L REV	Connecticut Law Review
CONT SOC	Contemporary Sociology
CORNELL LAW Q	Cornell Law Quarterly
CRIM JUS BEH	Criminal Justice and Behavior
CRIM L BULL	Criminal Law Bulletin
CRIM L Q	Criminal Law Quarterly
CRIM L REV	Criminal Law Review
CRIME & DELINQ	Crime and Delinquency Literature
CRIME AND SOC JUS	Crime and Social Justice
DAILY TELEGRAPH	Daily Telegraph
DE PAUL L REV	De Paul Law Review
DENVER L J	Denver Law Journal
DEUTSCH MED WSCHR	Deutsche Medizinische Wochenschrift
DEUTSCH Z GES GERICHTL MED	Deutsche Zeitschrift Für die Gesamte Gerichtliche Medizin now entitled Zeitschrift Für Rechtsmedizin/Journal of Legal Medicine
DIACRIT	Diacritics
DIMEN HEALTH SERV	Dimensions in Health Service
DISS ABST INTERNATL	Dissertation Abstracts International
DIV GOVT RES R (U N MEX)	New Mexico. University. Division of Government Research. Review
ECONOMIST	Economist
ED & PUB	Editor & Publisher
ED RE REPTS	Editorial Research Reports
EL GRITO DEL NORTE	El Grito Del Norte
EMER MED	Emergency Medicine
ENCOUNTER	Encounter
ENKE	ENKE's Bibliothek für Chemie und Technik unter Berücksichtigung der Volkswertschaft Stuttgart' 1, 1920+

ESQUIRE	Esquire
ETC	Etc
EVERYWOMAN	Everywoman
FAC L REV	Faculty of Law Review University of Toronto
FAM COORD	Family Coordinator
FBI L ENFORCE BULL	FBI Law Enforcement Bulletin
FED PROBAT	Federal Probation
FIFTH ESTATE	Fifth Estate
FOCUS-MIDWEST	Focus-Midwest
FORDHAM URBAN L J	Fordham Urban Law Journal
FORENSIC SCI	Forensic Science (Lausanne)
FREE NEWS	Free News
FREEDOMWAYS	Freedomways
GA L REV	Georgia Law Review
GA SB J	Georgia State Bar Journal
GAY	Gay
GAY LIBERATOR	Gay Liberator
GEO L J	Georgetown Law Journal
GEO WASH L REV	George Washington Law Review
GIDRA	Gidra
GOOD H	Good Housekeeping
GOOD TIMES	Good Times
GREAT SPECKLED BIRD	Great Speckled Bird
GUARDIAN	Guardian
HARP BAZ	Harper's Bazaar
HARRY	Harry
HARV J LEG	Harvard Journal on Legislation
HARV L REV	Harvard Law Review
HASTINGS L J	Hastings Law Journal
HERSELF	Herself
HEYTHROP J	Heythrop Journal
HOFSTRA L REV	Hofstra Law Review
HOSP	Hospitals
HOSP MED STAFF	Hospital Medical Staff
HOSP PHY	Hospital Physician

HOSP WORLD	Hospital World
HOSPITAL (Rio)	Hospital (Rio de Janeiro)
HOUSTON L REV	Houston Law Review
IA L REV	Iowa Law Review
ILL MED J	Illinois Medical Journal
IMPRINT	Imprint
IND L REV	Indiana Law Review
INTELLECT	Intellect
INTERNATL J CRIM & PENOL	International Journal of Criminology and Penology
ISS CRIM	Issues in Criminology
IT AIN'T ME BABE	It Ain't Me Babe
J ABNORM PSYCOL	Journal of Abnormal Psychology
J AM ACAD CHILD PSYCH	American Academy of Child Psychiatry. Journal
J AM COLL EMERGENCY PHYSICIANS	American College of Emergency Physicians. Journal
J AM FOLKLO	Journal of American Folklore
J AM MED ASS	American Medical Association. Journal
J AM MED WOM ASSOC	American Medical Women's Association Journal
J COMM PSYCHOL	Journal of Community Psychology
J CRIM JUS	Journal of Criminal Justice
J CRIM L, CRIMIN POLICE SCIENCE	*see* Journal of Criminal Law and Criminology
J CRIM LAW AND CRIM	Journal of Criminal Law and Criminology
J EMERGENCY NURS	JEN, Journal of Emergency Nursing
J FAM PRACT	Journal of Family Practice
J FAMILY L	Journal of Family Law
J FEM LIB	Journal of Female Liberation
J FL MED ASS	Florida Medical Association Journal
J FORENSIC SCI	Journal of Forensic Sciences
J GEN PSYCHOL	Journal of General Psychology
J HIST IDEAS	Journal of the History of Ideas
J LOUISIANA MED SOC	Journal of the Louisiana State Medical Society
J MARRIAGE	Journal of Marriage and the Family
J NATL ASSN WOMEN DEANS ADM & COUNSEL	National Association of Women Deans, Administrators and Counselors. Journal

J PASTORAL CARE	Journal of Pastoral Care
J PEDIAT	Journal of Pediatrics
J PER AND SOC PSYCHOLOGY	Journal of Personality and Social Psychology
J PHILIPP MED ASS	Philippine Medical Association. Journal
J POLIC SCI	Journal of Police Science and Administration
J PRACT NURS	Journal of Practical Nursing
J PSYCH & L	Journal of Psychiatry and Law
J PSYCHIAT NURSING MENT HEALTH SERV	Journal of Psychiatric Nursing and Mental Health Services formerly Journal of Psychiatric Nursing
J REL & HEALTH	Journal of Religion and Health
J REPROD MED	Journal of Reproductive Medicine
J SEX RES	Journal of Sex Research
J SOC HIST	Journal of Social History
J SOC ISSUES	Journal of Social Issues
J URBAN L	Journal of Urban Law
J UROL NEPHROL	Journal d'Urologie et de Nephrologie (Paris)
JOHN MARSHAL J	The John Marshall Journal of Practice and Procedure
JUDICATURE	Judicature
KHIRURGIIA	Khirurgiia (Sofiia)
L Q REV	Law Quarterly Review
LA L REV	Louisiana Law Review
LABOUR MO	Labour Monthly
LADDER	Ladder
LADIES HOME J	Ladies Home Journal
LAW QUART	Law Quarterly
LOOK	Look
LOYOLA L REV	Loyola Law Review
LOYOLA U L J	Loyola University Law Journal (Chicago)
MADEMOISELLE	Mademoiselle
MC CALLS	McCalls
MAJ REP	Majority Report
MAN L J	Manitoba Law Journal
MED ANN DC	Medical Annals of the District of Columbia

MED ASPECTS HUM SEXUAL	Medical Aspects of Human Sexuality
MED INSIGHT	Medical Insight
MED KLIN	Medizinische Klinik
MED LEG BULL	Medico-Legal Bulletin
MED LEG DOMM CORPOR	Medecine Legale et Dommage Corporel
MED SCI LAW	Medicine, Science and the Law
MED TIMES	Medical Times
MED TRIAL TECHN QUART	Medical Trial Technique Quarterly
MEDICOLEG J	Medico-Legal Journal
MENT HYG	M. H. (Mental Hygiene)
MICH L REV	Michigan Law Review
MILITANT	Militant
MINERVA MEDICOLEG	Minerva Medicolegale
MINN L REV	Minnesota Law Review
MISS LAW J	Mississippi Law Journal
MOD HEALTH CARE	Modern Health Care (New York)
MONTANA L REV	Montana Law Review
MS	Ms
MSCHR KRIMIN & STRAFRECHTSREFORM	Monatsschrift Für Kriminologie und Stra- frechtsreform

N C L REV	North Carolina Law Review
N Y MAG	New York Magazine
N Y SUNDAY NEWS	New York Sunday News
N Y TIMES	New York Times
N Y TIMES, ARTS & LEIS	New York Times, Arts & Leisure
N Y TIMES MAG	New York Times Magazine
N D L REV	North Dakota Law Review
NATION	Nation
NEB L REV	Nebraska Law Review
NED TIJDSCHR GENEESKD	Nederlands Tijdschrift voor Geneeskunde (Amsterdam)
NERVENARZT	Nervenarzt
NEW ENG J MED	New England Journal of Medicine
NEW ENGLAND L REV	New England Law Review
NEW HUMAN	New Humanist
NEW MEX L REV	New Mexico Law Review
NEW REP	New Republic

NEW SOC	New Society
NEW STATESM	New Statesman
NEW TIMES	New Times
NEWS FROM NOWHERE	News From Nowhere
NEWSDAY	Newsday
NEWSWK	Newsweek
NO MORE FUN AND GAMES	No More Fun and Games
NOLA EXPR	Nola Express
NORTHWEST PASS	Northwest Passage
NOVA	Nova
NURS CLIN NORTH AM	Nursing Clinics of North America
NURS DIGEST	Nursing Digest
NURS FORUM	Nursing Forum
NURS MIRROR	Nursing Mirror
NURS OUTLOOK	Nursing Outlook
NURSING RES	Nursing Research
NURSING '74	Nursing 1974
OBSERVER	Observer
OBSTET GYNECOL	Obstetrics and Gynecology
OLD MOLE	Old Mole
ORE L REV	Oregon Law Review
ORV HETIL	Orvosi Hetilap
OTHER WOMAN	Other Woman
OTTAWA L REV	Ottawa Law Review
PA MED	Pennsylvania Medicine
PEACE NEWS	Peace News
PEACEMAK	Peacemaker
PEDIATR CLIN NORTH AM	Pediatric Clinics of North America
PEOPLES WORLD	Peoples World
PERCEP & MOTOR SKILLS	Perceptual & Motor Skills
POLICE CHIEF	Police Chief
PRISM	Prism
PROGRESS	Progressive
PROGRESS WOMEN	Progressive Women
PROSPECTUS	Prospectus

PRZEGL LEK	Przeglad Lekarski
PRZEGLAD PENITENC-JARNY I KRYMINOL-OGICZNY	Przeglad Penitencjarny I Kryminologiczny
PSYCH STUDY OF THE CHILD	Psychoanalytic Study of the Child
PSYCHIATR NEUROL MED PSYCHOL	Psychiatrie, Neurologie und Medizinische Psychologie (Leipzig)
PSYCHOANAL Q	Psychoanalytic Quarterly
PSYCHOL REP	Psychological Reports
PSYCHOL TODAY	Psychology Today
PSYCHOS MED	Psychosomatic Medicine
PSYCHOTHER AND PSYCHOSOM	Psychotherapy and Psychosomatics
PSYCHOTHERAPY: THEORY RES & PRAC	Psychotherapy: Theory, Research and Practice
PUB HEALTH REP	Public Health Reports
QUEEN'S BAR BULL	Queen's Bar Bulletin (Queen's County Bar Association)
RAD THERAPIST	Radical Therapist
RAMP	Ramparts
RASS NEUROPSICHIATR	Rassegna di Neuropsichiatria (Salerno)
RAT	Rat
READ DIGEST	Reader's Digest
REDBK	Redbook
REGAN REP NURS	Regan Report on Nursing Law
REPORT	Reporter
RES STAFF PHYSICIAN	Resident and Staff Physician
REV NEUROPHYCHIAT INFANT	Revue de Neuropsychiatrie Infantile et d'Hygiene Mentale de l'Enfance (Paris)
RISING UP ANGRY	Rising Up Angry
RN	RN
S C L REV	South Carolina Law Review
SEC CITY	Second City
SEED	Seed
SEMIN PSYCH	Seminars in Psychiatry

SEVENTEEN	Seventeen
SEX ROLES	Sex Roles: A Journal of Research
SINGAPORE MED J	Singapore Medical Journal
SMITH COLL	Smith College Studies in Social Work
SO CALIF L REV	Southern California Law Review
SOC CASE	Social Casework
SOC ED	Social Education
SOC PROB	Social Problems
SOC WORK	Social Work (United States)
SOCIALMED T	Socialmedicinsk Tidskrift
SOCIOL RUR	Sociologia Ruralis
SOUTH MED J	Southern Medical Journal
SOUTH PAT	Southern Patriot
SPECTATOR	Spectator
SPEECH TEAC	Speech Teacher
SRPSKI ARH CELOK LEK	Srpski Arhiv za Celokupno Lekarstvo
ST JOHN'S L REV	St. John's Law Review
ST LOUIS OUTLAW	St. Louis Outlaw
STAN L REV	Stanford Law Review
SUD MED EKSPERT	Sudebno-Meditsinskaia Ekspertiza (Moskva)
SUFFOLK U L REV	Suffolk University Law Review
SYRACUSE L REV	Syracuse Law Review

TAKEOVER	Takeover
TASMANIA U L R	Tasmania University Law Review
TEX L REV	Texas Law Review
TEX TECH L REV	Texas Tech Law Review
THE SEC WAVE	The Second Wave
TIME	Time
TODAYS HEALTH	Today's Health
TR LAW Q	Trial Lawyer's Quarterly
TRIAL	Trial
TUL L REV	Tulane Law Review
TULSA L J	Tulsa Law Journal

U CHI L REV	University of Chicago Law Review
U CIN L REV	University of Cincinnati Law Review
U COLO L REV	University of Colorado Law Review
U FLA L REV	University of Florida Law Review
U MICH J L REF	University of Michigan Journal of Law Reform

U PA LAW R	University of Pennsylvania Law Review
U RICH L REV	University of Richmond Law Review
U S NEWS	U. S. News and World Report
U TOL LAW R	University of Toledo Law Review
UBC L REV	University of British Columbia Law Review
UMKC L REV	UMKC Law Review
VA L REV	Virginia Law Review
VA MED MON	Virginia Medical Monthly
VAL U L REV	Valparaiso University Law Review
VAND L REV	Vanderbilt Law Review
VILLAGE VOICE	Village Voice
VOGUE	Vogue
W & M L REV	William & Mary Law Review
W BRIDGE	Willamette Bridge
W VA L REV	West Virginia Law Review
WALL ST J	Wall Street Journal
WASH & LEE L REV	Washington & Lee Law Review
WASH M	Washington Monthly
WASH U L Q	Washington University Law Quarterly
WASHBURN L J	Washburn Law Journal
WAYNE L REV	Wayne Law Review
WEST J MED	Western Journal of Medicine
WIEN KLIN WSCHR	Wiener Klinische Wochenschrift
WILLAMETTE L J	Willamette Law Journal
WIN	Win
WOMBAT	Wombat
WOMEN: A J OF LIB	Women: A Journal of Liberation
WOMEN LAW J	Women Lawyers Journal
WOMEN SPEAKING	Women Speaking
WOMENS PRESS	Womens Press
WOMEN'S WORLD	Women's World
WORK WORLD	Workers World
YALE L J	Yale Law Journal
ZACCHIA	Zacchia

SUBJECT HEADINGS USED IN THIS
BIBLIOGRAPHY

ABORTION
ACQUITTAL
AGGRAVATED RAPE
ALCOHOL AND ALCOHOLISM
ALLEGED RAPE
ANTI RAPE
APPEAL

BERG ACID PHOSPHATASE
  TEST
BIBLIOGRAPHY
BIOFEEDBACK TREATMENT
BIRTH CONTROL
BOOK EXCERPTS
BOOK REVIEWS

CAPITAL PUNISHMENT
CASTRATION
CAUTIONARY INSTRUCTION
CHILD RAPE
CONFERENCES
CONSENT
CONVICTION
CORROBORATION
CRIME RATE
CRIMINOLOGY

DEFLORATION
DRUG TREATMENT

EROTIC STIMULI
EVIDENCE

FEMINISM
FORCIBLE RAPE
FRAUD

GANG RAPE

HEILBRUN
HISTORY
HITCHIKERS
HOSPITAL EMERGENCY ROOMS
HOSPITALS
HOSPITALS—RAPE IN
HYMEN

JUVENILE OFFENDERS

LAWS AND LEGISLATION

TABLE OF CONTENTS

BOOKS

A

Alabama. Governor's Commission to Study Sex Offenses. INTERIM REPORT. Birmingham: The Commission, 1967.

Amir, Menachem. PATTERNS IN FORCIBLE RAPE. Chicago: University of Chicago Press, 1971.

Astor, Gerald. THE CHARGE IS RAPE. Chicago: Playboy Press, 1974.

—. A QUESTION OF RAPE. New York: Pinnacle Books, 1974.

B

Bailey, Francis Lee and Henry B. Rothblatt. CRIMES OF VIOLENCE. Rochester, New York: Lawyers Co-operative Publishing Company, 1973.

—. RAPE AND OTHER SEX CRIMES. Volume Two, 1975.

Baughman, Laurence E. Alan. SOUTHERN RAPE COMPLEX: HUNDRED YEAR PSYCHOSIS. Atlanta: Pendulum Books, 1966.

Berger, Peter L. and Brigitte Berger. SOCIOLOGY: A BIO-GRAPHICAL APPROACH. New York: Basic Books, 1972.

Brandtson, Garth. KIDNAPPED, RAPED AND HUMILIATED.

np: Barclay House, 1974.

Brongersma, Edward. SEX EN STRAF: 's-Gravenhage: NVSH, 1970.

Brownmiller, Susan. AGAINST OUR WILL: MEN, WOMEN AND RAPE. New York: Simon and Schuster, 1975.

Burgess, Ann Wolbert and Lynda Lytle Holmstrom. RAPE: VICTIMS OF CRISIS. Bowie, Maryland: R. J. Brady Company, 1974.

C

California. Department of Mental Hygiene. Louise V. Frisbie. ANOTHER LOOK AT SEX OFFENDERS IN CALIFORNIA. Research Monograph Number 12. Sacramento: The Department, 1969.

—. Department of Mental Hygiene. Bureau of Research and Statistics. Louise V. Frisbie and Ernest H. Dondis. RECIDIVISM AMONG TREATED SEX OFFENDERS. Research Monograph Number 5. Sacramento: The Bureau, 1965.

—. Langley Porter Neuropsychiatric Institute, San Francisco. FINAL REPORT ON CALIFORNIA SEXUAL DEVIATION RESEARCH. Sacramento: The Institute, 1954.

—. Legislature. Assembly Committee on Criminal Justice. REVISING CALIFORNIA LAWS RELATING TO RAPE: TRANSCRIPT OF THE HEARING BEFORE THE ASSEMBLY CRIMINAL JUSTICE COMMITTEE AND THE CALIFORNIA COMMISSION ON THE STATUS OF WOMEN; LOS ANGELES, OCTOBER 18, 1973. np: 1974.

Center for Women Policy Studies. RAPE, by Carol Vidaros, with an introduction by Jody Pinto and with a nationwide directory of U. S. rape crisis centers. New Canaan, Connecticut: Tobey Publishing Comapny, 1974.

—. RAPE AND IT VICTIMS: A REPORT FOR CITIZENS,

2

HEALTH FACILITIES AND CRIMINAL JUSTICE AGEN-
CIES, by Lisa Brodyaga, et al. Washington DC: National Institute of Law Enforcement and Criminal Justice, 1975.

Chappell, Duncan and Susan Singer. RAPE IN NEW YORK
CITY: A STUDY OF MATERIAL IN THE POLICE FILES
AND ITS MEANING. Albany, New York: State University
of New York, 1973.

Clark, Joseph S., et al. CRIME IN URBAN SOCIETY. Edited
by Barbara N. McLennan. New York: Dunellen, 1970.

Coote, Anna and Tess Gill. RAPE: THE CONTROVERSY, THE
LAW, THE MYTHS, THE FACTS: CHANGES THAT ARE
NEEDED AND WHAT TO DO IF IT HAPPENS TO YOU.
London: National Council for Civil Liberties, 1975.

Crescenti, Giovanni. LA CONDANNA ALLO STUPRO DELLE
VERGINI CRISTIANE DURANTE LE PERSECUZIONI
DELL 'AMPERO ROMANO. Palermo: Flaccavio, 1966.

Csida, June Bundy and Joseph Csida. RAPE; HOW TO AVOID
IT AND WHAT TO DO ABOUT IT IF YOU CAN'T. Chats-
worth, California: Books for Better Living, 1974.

D

De Francis, Vincent. PROTECTING THE CHILD VICTIM OF
SEX CRIMES COMMITTED BY ADULTS: FINAL RE-
PORT. Denver: American Humane Association, Children's
Division, 1969.

Delva, J. AANRANDING VAN DE EERBAARHEID EN VER-
KRACHTING. Brussel: Huis Ferdinand Larcier, 1967.

DeRiver, Joseph Paul. CRIME AND THE SEXUAL PSYCHO-
PATH. Springfield, Illinois: C. C. Thomas, 1958.

Detroit. Police Department. Women's and Children's Service
Section. RAPE: A BRIEF PROFILE, DETROIT, MICHI-
GAN, 1974. Detroit: The Department, 1974.

Dieckhoff, Albrecht Diedrich. ZUR RECHTSLAGE IM DER-ZEITIGEN SITTENSTRAFRECHT. Hamburg: Kriminalistik, Verlag fur Kriminalistische Fachliteratur, 1958.

Dietrich, Eckhart. WIEDERHOLUNGSGEFAHR BEI SITT-LICHKEITSVERBRECHEN. Berlin: Duncker and Humblot, 1970.

Drzazga, John. SEX CRIMES. Springfield, Illinois: C. C. Thomas, 1960.

Duffy, Clinton T. and Al Hirshberg. SEX AND CRIME. Garden City: Doubleday, 1965.

E

Eliade, Mircea. MEPHISTOPHELES AND THE ANDROGYNE; STUDIES IN RELIGIOUS MYTH AND SYMBOL. Translated by J. M. Cohen. New York: Sheed and Ward, 1965.

G

Gager, Nancy and Cathleen Scurr. SEXUAL ASSAULT: CONFRONTING RAPE IN AMERICA. New York: Grosset and Dunlap, 1976.

Gebbard, P. H., et al. SEX OFFENDERS: AN ANALYSIS OF TYPES. New York: np: 1965.

Gerbener, Hermann. DIE KRIMINALITAT DER KINDER-SCHANDUNG IM LANDGERICHTSBEZIRK DUISBURG IN DEN JAHREN 1950-1954. Köln, Spezialdruckerei fur Dissertationen: Gouder V. Hansen, 1965.

Goldberg, Jacob Alter and Rosamond W. Goldberg. GIRLS ON CITY STREETS; A STUDY OF 1400 CASES OF RAPE. New York: Arno Press, 1974.

H

Hanack, Ernst Walter. ZUR REVISION DES SEXUALSTRAF-
RECHTS IN DER BUNDESREPUBLIK; EIN RECHTS-
GUTACHTEN UNTER MITARBEIT VON E. WAHLE UND
J. v. GERLACH. Reinbek bei Hamburg: Rowohlt, 1969.

Herschberger, Ruth. ADAM'S RIB. New York: Har/Row
Books, 1970.

Hyde, Margaret Oldroyd. SPEAK OUT ON RAPE. New York:
McGraw Hill, 1976.

I

Illinois. Commission on Sex Offenders. A REPORT TO THE
74th GENERAL ASSEMBLY AND THE GOVERNOR:
THE HONORABLE OTTO KERNER. Evanston: The Commission, 1965.

Indiana, University. Institute for Sex Research. SEX OFFEND-
ERS: AN ANALYSIS OF TYPES, by Paul H. Gebherd,
et al. New York: Harper and Row, 1965.

Inglis, Amirah. NOT A WHITE WOMAN SAFE: SEXUAL
ANXIETY AND POLITICS IN PORT MORESBY, 1920-
1934. Canberra: Australian National University Press, 1974.

K

Kling, Samuel G. SEXUAL BEHAVIOR AND THE LAW. New
York: Bernard Geis Associates; distributed by Random
House, 1965.

Koops, J. A., et al. DELICTEN BETREFFENDE DE SEK-
SUALITEIT. Deventer: A. E. Kluwer, 1968.

L

Langeluddeke, Albrecht. DIE ENTMANNUNG VON SITTLICH-KEITSVERBRECHERN. Berlin: De Gruyter, 1963.

Lucas, Norman. THE SEX KILLERS. New York: W. H. Allen, 1974.

Lynch, W. Ware. RAPE! ONE VICTIM'S STORY: A DOCU-MENTARY. Chicago: Follett Publishing Company, 1974.

M

Macdonald, John Marshall. RAPE OFFENDERS AND THEIR VICTIMS. With a chapter by Hunter S. Thompson. Springfield, Illinois: Thomas, 1971.

MacKellar, Jean Scott. RAPE: THE BAIT AND THE TRAP. New York: Crown Publishers, 1975.

Masters, Robert E. and Eduard Lea. SEX CRIMES IN HISTORY; EVOLVING CONCEPTS OF SADISM, LUST-MURDER, AND NECROPHILIA: FROM ANCIENT TO MODERN TIMES. New York: Julian Press, 1963.

Medea, Andra and Kathleen Thompson. AGAINST RAPE. New York: Farrar, Straus, and Giroux, 1974.

Mendoza Duran, Jose O. EL DELITO DE VIOLACION. Barcelona, 1962.

Meyers, David W. THE HUMAN BODY AND THE LAW; A MEDICO-LEGAL STUDY. Chicago, Aldine Publishing Company, 1970.

Minnesota. Department of Corrections. Section on Research and Statistics. THE SEX OFFENDER IN MINNESOTA. Nathan G. Mandel, director of research. St. Paul: The Department, 1964.

Mohr, J. W. SEXUAL BEHAVIOR AND THE CRIMINAL LAW

PRELIMINARY REPORT. Toronto, 1965.

Montarron, Marcel. HISTOIRE DES CRIMES SEXUELS. Paris: Plon, 1970.

Morland, Nigel. AN OUTLINE OF SEXUAL CRIMINOLOGY. Oxford: Tallis Publishing Company, 1966.

N

National League of Cities. RAPE/NATIONAL LEAGUE OF CITIES, UNITED STATES CONFERENCE OF MAYORS. Washington DC: The League and the Conference, 1974.

New York Radical Feminists. RAPE: THE FIRST SOURCE-BOOK FOR WOMEN, edited by Noreen Connell and Cassandra Wilson. New York: New American Library, 1974.

Niemann, Harold. UNZUCHT MIT KINDERN: EINE KRIMIN-OLOGISCHE UNTERSUCHUNG UNTER VERWENDUNG HAMBURGER GERICHTSAKTEN AUS DEN JAHREN, 1965 und 1967. np: nd.

Norman, Eve. RAPE. Los Angeles: Wollstonecraft Incorporated, 1973.

O

Oliver, Bernard J. SEXUAL DEVIATION IN AMERICAN SOCIETY: A SOCIAL PSYCHOLOGICAL STUDY OF SEXUAL NON-CONFORMITY. New Haven, 1967.

P

Parker, Tony. THE HIDDEN WORLD OF SEX OFFENDERS, formerly entitled THE TWISTING LAND: SOME SEX OFFENDERS. London: Panther, 1970. Indianapolis, Bobbs-Merril, 1969.

Pekkanen, John. VICTIMS: AN ACCOUNT OF A RAPE. New York: Dial Press, 1976.

Penagos, Gustavo. ASPECTO CANONICO DEL DELITO DE ESTUPRO; COLISION DE LEYES CANONICAS, CIVILES Y CONCORDATARIES. Bogota: Impreso en los Talleres de la Editorial Prag, 1967.

Pennsylvania. Commission for Women. HELP FOR THE RAPE VICTIM. Harrisburg: The Commission, 1975.

—. Commission on the Status of Women. REPORT. Harrisburg: The Commission, 1973.

Plaut, Paul. DER SEXUALVERBRECHER UND SEINE PERSONLICHKEIT. np: Enke, 1960.

Porte-Petit Candaudap, Celestino. ENSAYO DOGMATICO SOBRE EL DELITO DE VIOLACION. Mexico: Editorial Juridica Mexicana, 1966.

Pacific Sociological Association. RAPE AS A FALSE ISSUE IN THE LIBERATION MOVEMENT, a paper presented by Cecile Baril and Iain Couchman. Scottsdale, Arizona: The Association, 1973.

R

Readers Advisory Service. BIBLIOGRAPHY: RAPE, by Doris F. Kaplan. np: Science Associates International, 1975.

Reinhardt, Heinz. DIE BESTRAFUNG DER UNZUCHT MIT KINDERN UNTER BESONDERER BERUCKSICHTIGUNG DES VERHALTENS UND DER PERSONLICHKEIT DES OPFERS. Bern, Stuttgart: Haupt, 1967.

Rogers, Kenneth Paul. FOR ONE SWEET GRAPE: THE EXTRAORDINARY MEMOIR OF A CONVICTED RAPIST/MURDERER. Chicago: Playboy Press, 1974.

Roucek, Joseph Stanley. SEXUAL ATTACK AND THE CRIME

OF RAPE. Charlottesville, New York: Sam Har Press, 1975.

Russell, Diana E. H. THE POLITICS OF RAPE; THE VICTIM'S PERSPECTIVE. New York: Stein and Day, 1975.

S

Sagarin, Edward. PROBLEMS OF SEX BEHAVIOR. New York: Crowell, 1968.

Sanctuary, Gerald. SEXUALITY AND VIOLENCE. New York: Sex Information and Education Council of the United States, Incorporated, 1970.

Scacco, Anthony M. RAPE IN PRISON. Springfield, Illinois: C. C. Thomas, 1975.

Schaeffer, Max Pierre. DER TRIEBTATER. Munchen: Lichtenberg-Verlag, 1970.

Schultz, Gladys. HOW MANY MORE VICTIMS? Philadelphia: Lippincott, 1965.

Schultz, LeRoy G. RAPE VICTIMOLOGY. Springfield, Illinois: C. C. Thomas, 1974.

Schmid, Hans. SEXUALSTRAFRECHT. Lubeck: Verlag für Polizeiliches Fachschrifttum, 1970.

Schnetz, Heinz. DAS KIND ALS KLASSISCHER ZEUGE BEI SEXUALDELIKTEN. Darmstadt: N. Stoytscheff, 1960.

Schonfelder, Thea. DIE ROLLE DES MADCHENS BEI SEXUALDELIKTEN. Stuttgart: Enke, 1968.

Seattle, Washington. Law and Justice Planning Office. FORCIBLE RAPE IN SEATTLE, 1973. Seattle: The Office, 1974.

Sedlacek, William E., et al. DIFFERENCES IN RACIAL ATTITUDES OF WHITE MALES AND FEMALES. np: Eric, 1972.

9

Slater, Manning R. SEX OFFENDERS IN GROUP THERAPY. Los Angeles: Sherbourne Press, 1964.

Slovenko, Ralph. SEXUAL BEHAVIOR AND THE LAW. Springfield, Illinois: Thomas, 1965.

Smith, Arthur Robert and James V. Giles. AN AMERICAN RAPE: A TRUE ACCOUNT OF THE GILES-JOHNSON CASE. Washington: New Republic Book Company, 1975.

Storaska, Frederic. HOW TO SAY NO TO A RAPIST AND SURVIVE. New York: Random House, 1975.

Sturup, Georg Kristoffer. TREATMENT OF SEXUAL OF-FENDERS IN HERSTEDVESTER: DENMARK. Copenhagen, Munksgaard, 1968.

T

Tabori, Paul. THE SOCIAL HISTORY OF RAPE. London: New England Library, 1971.

Theede, Peter. UNZUCHT MIT ABHANGIGEN. Lubeck: Schmidt-Romhild, 1967.

W

Wahle, Eberhard. ZUR REFORM DES SEXUALSTRAF RE-CHTS. Frankfurt am Main: A. Metzner, 1969.

Weiss, Carl and David James Friar. TERROR IN THE PRISONS: HOMOSEXUAL RAPE AND WHY SOCIETY CONDONES IT. Indianapolis: Bobbs-Merrill, 1974.

Winslow, Robert Wallace and Virginia Winslow. DEVIANT REALITY: ALTERNATIVE WORLD VIEWS. Boston: Allyn and Bacon, 1974.

Wisconsin. Legislative Reference Bureau. RAPE LAW RE-VISION: A BRIEF SUMMARY OF STATE ACTION.

Madison: The Burearu, 1975.

Wood, Jim. THE RAPE OF INEZ GARCIA. New York: Putnam, 1976.

PERIODICAL LITERATURE BY TITLE

Abolishing cautionary instructions in sex offense cases. People v. Rincon-Pineda. CRIM L BULL 12:58-72, January, 1976.

Abortion in case of rape and the code of medical ethics, by L. Ribeiro. HOSPITAL (Rio) 67:9-19, January, 1965.

Accountability: a right of the rape victim, by A. W. Burgess, et al. J PSYCHIAT NURSING MENT HEALTH SERV 13:11-16, May-June, 1975.

Accountability and rights of rape victim, by A. W. Burgess, et al. AM J ORTHOP 44(2):182, 1974.

Adequecy of ego functioning in rapists and pedophiles, by T. K. Seghorn. DISS ABST INTERNATL 31(12-B):7613-7614, June, 1971.

Admissibility of a rape-complainant's previous sexual conduct: the need for legislative reform. NEW ENGLAND L REV 11: 497-507, Spring, 1976.

Aftermath of rape, by W. H. Masters, et al. REDBK 147:74+, June, 1976.

Afterthoughts on the morning-after pill, by K. Weiss. MS 2:5, November, 1973.

Against our will—men, women and rape, by S. Brownmiller. A review by S. Ardener. NEW SOC 34(687):556-557, 1975.

—. A review by J. Stafford. ESQUIRE 84:50+, November,

1975.

—. A review by J. Howard. MADEMOISELLE 82:6, January, 1976.

—. A review by H. E. Schwartz. NATION 221:556-558, November, 1975.

Age of the culprits and the injured in sex offenses, by I. Klose. DEUTSCH Z GES GERICHTL MED 59:129-134, 1967.

Aggravated rape, by L. J. Walinsky. NEW REP 173(3):32.

Alcohol and forcible rape, by M. Amir. BRIT J ADDICT 62: 219-232, December, 1967.

Alcoholism and forcible rape, by R. T. Rada. AM J PSYCH 132:444-446, April, 1975.

Alleged rape, an invitational symposium. J REPROD MED 12: 133-144, April, 1974.

Anatomy of a rape. ST. LOUIS OUTLAW 1(14):5, March, 1971.

Another look at the care of the rape victim, by J. W. Hanss, Jr. ARIZ MED 32(8):634-635, August, 1975.

Another rape frameup. SOUTH PAT 32(4):5, April, 1974.

Antirape, by Hoffman. ANN ARBOR SUN 2(8):5, April 19, 1974.

Antirape package raped, by Hoffman. ANN ARBOR SUN 2(7): 6, April 5, 1974.

Antirape proposal gains support, by Hoffman. ANN ARBOR SUN 2(6):11, March 22, 1974.

Anti-rape technique: interview, by S. Brownmiller. HARP BAZ 109:119+, March, 1976.

Apathy/word of a gentleman, by Williams. MAJ REP 4(9):3, August 22, 1974.

Appeal of Carrington Case, by Lewis. WORK WORLD 16(7): 14, April 5, 1974.

Application of a dye used in histology for the purpose of identification of spermatozoids in sperm stains on fabrics, by G. Squillaci. ACTA MED LEG SOC 17:69-70, April-June, 1964.

Arrest feminist at rapists trial, by Kearon. EVERYWOMAN 2 (15):7, October 26, 1971.

Aspects of rape, by K. Lindsey, et al. THE SEC WAVE 2:2.

Assessing trauma in the rape victim, by L. L. Holmstrom, et al. AM J NURSING 75:1288-1291, August, 1975.

An Atlanta antirape program, by Krista. GREAT SPECKLED BIRD 7(37):6, September 16, 1974.

Atlanta rallies against rape, by Dace. GREAT SPECKLED BIRD 7(34):4, August 26, 1974.

Attack on women, by J. H. Court. AUSTRALAS NURSES J 4:1+, September, 1975.

Attribution of fault to a rape victim as a function of respectability of the victim, by C. Jones, et al. J PER AND SOC PSYCHOLOGY 26(3):415-419, June, 1973.

Avoiding rape: whose advice should you take? by N. Gittelson. MC CALLS 103:66, May, 1976.

Battery and rape; medico-ethical problems in the examination and reporting to the police, by H. T. Cremers. NED TIJD-SCHR GENEESKD 119(32):1259-1262, August 9, 1975.

Been down so long. SEED 6(10):5, April 7, 1971.

The behind-the-scenes story of the unanimous repeal bill victory, by N. Leurs. MAJ REPT 3:6-7, March, 1974.

Being an Asian in Texas, worth 20 years. PEOPLES WORLD 34 (21):8, May 22, 1971.

Beware of female hitchikers, by Wicker. GAY 2(45):4, March 1, 1971.

Bibliography of hospital emergency departments and trauma units—organization and management, by J. Ryan. BULL AM COLL SURG 60:17-20, September, 1975.

Big-house rape—cases, causes and cures, by G. M. Farkas. FED PROBAT 39(4):62, 1975.

Bikers get death sentence. ADVOCATE 41:A1, July 3, 1974.

Biofeedback treatment of a rape related psychophysiological cardiovascular disorder, by G. G. Abel, et al. PSYCHOS MED 37(1):85, 1975.

Black charged with raping white, by Grant. SOUTH PAT 29(8): 6, October, 1971.

Black man, white woman—the maintenance of a myth: rape and the press in New Orleans, by D. J. Abbott, et al., in CRIME AND DELINQUENCY, by M. Riedel. Praeger, 1974, pp. 141-153.

Bringing the rapist to trial, a group effort, by C. Price. WOMEN'S WORLD 1:3, November-December, 1971.

But what do we do with our rage? by G. Steinem. MS 3:51, May, 1975.

California rape evidence reform: an analysis of Senate bill 1678. HASTINGS L J 26:1551-1573, May, 1975.

Can a black be acquitted? Indictment of R. Holloway, by N. C. Chriss. NATION 211:690-691, December 28, 1970.

Caryatid: war, rape and masculine consciousness, by A. Rich.

AM POETRY REV 2:10-11, May-June, 1973.

The case against Steven Truscott in Canada, by K. Simpson. MEDICOLEG J 36:suppl, 4:58-71, 1968.

Case contribution to the problem of castration of sex offenders hospitalized in a provincial hospital according to paragraph 42b of the German Penal Code, by H. Neumann. NERVENARZT 39:369-375, August, 1968.

A case of Heller's dementia following sexual assault in a four-year-old girl, by C. Koupernik, et al. CHILD PSYCH AND HUM DEV 2(3):134-144, Spring, 1972.

Case that could end capital punishment: Maxwell vs Bishop, by R. Hammer. N Y TIMES MAG 46-47+, October 12, 1969.

Centenary reflections in Prince's case, by R. Cross. L Q REV 91:540-553, October, 1975.

Certification of rape under the Colorado abortion statute. U COLO L REV 42:121, May, 1970.

Characteristics of rape victims seen in crisis-intervention, by S. L. McCombie. SMITH COLL 46(2):137-158, 1976.

Chicana rape victim fights indictment. BLACK PANTH 12(4):9, August 17, 1974.

Child rape: defusing a psychological time bomb, by J. J. Peters. HOSP PHY 9:46-49, February, 1973.

Children who were raped, by A. Katan. PSYCH STUDY OF THE CHILD 28:208-224, 1973.

Clinical and research impressions regarding murder and sexually perverse crimes, by L. M. Howell. PSYCHOTHER AND PSYCHOSOM 21(106):156-159, 1972-1973.

Clinical study of "plots" (sex crimes committed by gangs), by P.

Parrot, et al. REV NEUROPSYCHIAT INFANT 11:385-390, July-August, 1963.

Code R, for rape. NEWSWK 80:75, November 13, 1972.

Coming out of dark ages, by Hing. ANN ARBOR SUN 2(2):10, January 25, 1974.

Community supports condemned men. SOUTH PAT 32(2):1, February, 1974.

A conference on rape, by Blakkan. RAD THERAPIST 2(2):6, September, 1971.

Conference on rape. EVERYWOMAN 2(9):2, June 18, 1971.

Consciousness-raising on rape and violence, by J. Walker. WOMBAT 1:1, February, 1972.

Consent and responsibility in sexual offenses, by K. L, Koh. CRIM L REV 150-162, March, 1968.

Considerations on the subject of defloration, by G. Faraone, et al. ZACCHIA 7:101-118, January-March, 1971.

Constitutional law: capital punishment for rape constitutes cruel and unusual punishment when no life is taken or endangered. MINN L REV 56:95, November, 1971.

Constitutional law—cruel and unusual punishment. SUFFOLK U L REV 5:504, Winter, 1971.

Constitutional law—death penalty as cruel and unusual punishment for rape. W & M L REV 12:682, Spring, 1971.

Constitutional law—the eighth amendment's proscription of cruel and unusual punishment precludes imposition of the death sentence for rape when the victim's life is neither taken nor endangered. GEO WASH L REV 40:161, October, 1971.

Constitutional law—the Texas equal rights amendment—a rape statute that only punishes men does not violate the Texas

ERA. TEX TECH L REV 7:724-731, Spring, 1976.

Constitutionality of the death penalty for non-aggravated rape. WASH U L Q 1972:170, Winter, 1972.

Convenient suspect/murder/rape case. SOUTH PAT 32(7):6, September, 1974.

Conviction of secondary party for rape where principal acquitted, by J. R. Scott. LAW QUART 91:364):478-482, 1975.

Coping behavior of the rape victim, by A. W. Burgess, et al. AM J PSYCH 133:413-418, April, 1976.

Coping with crime. CHR TODAY 19:30-31, January 6, 1975.

Correction, by Bendor. GAY LIBERATOR 40:15, September, 1974.

Corroborating charges of rape. COLUM L REV 67:1137, June, 1967.

Corroboration in rape cases in New York—a half step forward, by A. B. Goldstein. ALBANY LAW R 37(2):306-328, 1972-1973.

The corroboration rule and crimes accompanying a rape. U PA LAW R 118(3):458-472, 1970.

Counseling rape victims, by Rev. R. S. Crum. J PASTORAL CARE 28:112-121, June, 1974.

Couple-speak: rape, true and false, by S. de Gramont, et al. VOGUE 157:108+, June, 1971.

Court changes rape penalty. SOUTH PAT 29(1):7, January, 1971.

Crime of rape, by H. B. Shaffer. ED RES REPTS 43-60, January 19, 1972.

The crime of rape in the Albuquerque area, by B. Turpen.

DIV GOVT RES R (U N MEX) 83:1-4, January, 1975.

Crimes of violence—rape and other sex crimes, by F. L. Bailey and H. B. Rothblatt. A review by A. S. Cordon. MISS LAW J 46(3):549-552, 1975.

—. A review by J. R. Galvin. U TOL LAW REV 6(2):570-571, 1975.

The criminal code and rape and sex offenses, by V. A. Lindabury. CAN NURSE 71(4):3, April, 1975.

Criminal law: mistake of age as a defense to statutory rape. U FLA L REV 18:699, Spring, 1966.

Criminal law—prosecution for assault with intent to rape is permissable even after a prior acquittal for rape, and a present intent to rape in the future completes the offense. TEX L REV 51:360, January, 1973.

Criminal law—psychiatric examination of prosecutrix in rape case. NC L REV 45:234, December, 1966.

Criminal law—rape—cautionary instruction in sex offense trial relating prosecutrix's credibility to the nature of the crime charged is no longer mandatory; discretionary use is disapproved. FORDHAM URBAN L J 4:419-430, Winter, 1976.

Criminal law—rape—death penalty—eighth amendment prohibition against cruel and unusual punishments forbids execution when the victim's life was neither taken nor endangered. U CIN L REV 40:396, Summer, 1971.

Criminal procedure—instruction to jury that rape is easy to charge and difficult to disprove is no longer to be given. TEX TECH L REV 7:732-737, Spring, 1976.

Criminal sexual conduct law passes, by Crandell. ANN ARBOR SUN 2(15):4, July 26, 1974.

Criminal violence: inquiries into national patterns and behavior. DISS ABST INTERNATL 33(12-A):7052, June, 1973.

Crisis and counseling requests of rape victims, by A. W. Burgess, et al. NURSING RES 23:196-202, May-June, 1974.

Crisis intervention and investigation of forcible rape, by M. Bard, et al. POLICE CHIEF 41(5):68-74, 1974.

Crisis intervention in the emergency room for rape victims, by Rev. H. R. Lewis. BULL AM PROTE HOSP ASS 37(2):112-119, 1973.

Crisis intervention with victims of rape, by S. S. Fox, et al. SOC WORK 17(1):37-42, January, 1972.

Critical disorders of sex behavior in temporal epilepsy, by G. D'Agata, et al. RASS NEUROPSICHIATR 22:191-204, April-June, 1968.

Cruel and unusual punishment—constitutionality of the death penalty for rape where victim's life neither taken nor endangered. U RICH L REV 5:392, Spring, 1971.

Cultural and sexual differences on the judgement of criminal offenses: a replication study of the measurement of delinquency, by M. Hsu. J CRIM LAW AND CRIM 64(3):349-353, 1973.

D.P.P. vs Morgan. 2 W L R 913. L Q REV 91:478-482, October, 1975.

Daylight prowlers, by J. Steele. GUARDIAN 11, November 26, 1975.

Deadly sex games in prison, by Dennis. ADVOCATE 44:25, August 14, 1974.

Dealing with rape, by H. Newman. THE SEC WAVE 2:3.

Dear bridge women and all women. W BRIDGE 4(22):2, June 3, 1971.

Death penalty for rape. NATION 200:156-157, February 15, 1965.

21

Defending yourself against rape: excerpts from *Our Bodies, Ourselves.* LADIES HOME J 90:62+, July, 1973.

Defloration. Answer to observations of Prof. Uribe Cualla, by G. Faraone, et al. ZACCHIA 8:7-10, January-March, 1972.

Demonstration of spermatozoa in the vaginal smear after criminal assault, by W. Spann. DEUTSCH Z GES GERICHTL MED 55:184-185, September 1, 1964.

DES: Banned for cattle and prescribed for women, by E. Frankfort. VILLAGE VOICE 7, March 22, 1973.

Development of a medical-center rape crisis-intervention program, by S. L. McCombie. AM J PSYCH 133(4):418-421, 1976.

Dirt in dogpatch/Al Capp and kids. COLL PRESS SER 10:9, November 3, 1971.

Disarm rapists. NEWS FROM NOWHERE 3(3):14, November 3, 1970.

—. IT AIN'T ME BABE 1(15):13, October 8, 1970.

—. IT AIN'T ME BABE 1(10):13, July 23, 1970.

Disposition of juvenile offenders, by B. Green. CRIM L Q 13:348, June, 1971.

Dispute over care of Baltimore County rape victims settled; hospitals to be paid. AM MED NEWS 18:12, August 11, 1975.

Do all Filipino women have lacerated hymens? by P. Anzures. J PHILIPP MED ASS 40:763-764, September, 1964.

Do rape victims get what they deserve? NEW HUMAN 89:314, January, 1974.

Don't take it lying down, by C. W. Offir. PSYCHOL TODAY 8:73, January, 1975.

Drunkenness as a defense to rape: R. vs Vandervoort (O W N 141) and R. vs Boucher (2 C C C 241). FAC L REV 22:133, April, 1964.

The effect in Philadelphia of Pennsylvania's increased penalties for rape and attempted rape, by B. Schwartz. J CRIM L, CRIMIN POLICE SCIENCE 59(4):509-515, December, 1968.

Emergency department protocol for management of rape cases, by C. R. Hayman, et al. J AM MED ASS 226:1577-1578, December 24-31, 1973.

Establishment of a rape crisis center, by G. E. Robinson, et al. CAN MENT HEALTH 23(5):10-12, September, 1975.

Estrogen therapy after rape? by B. Paulshock, et al. ANN INTERN MED 72:961, June, 1970.

Eugene procedure for rape victims, by Parker. WOMENS PRESS 1(9):11, October, 1971.

Evaluation and differentiation of the penal responsibility of the sex offender, by H. Hinderer. PSYCHIATR NEUROL MED PSYCHOL 25:257-265, May, 1973.

Evidence—admissibility—in a trial for rape, prosecutrix may not be cross examined as to specific acts of prior sexual conduct with men other than defendant, whether the purpose of such cross-examination is to establish her consent as an affirmative defense or to impeach her credibility as a witness. GA L REV 8:973-983, Summer, 1974.

Evidence—criminal law—prior sexual offenses against a person other than the prosecutrix. TUL L REV 46:336, December, 1971.

Evidence of complainant's sexual conduct in rape cases, by G. Zucker. BROOK BARR 27:55-65, November, 1975.

Evidence—presumption that trial judge disregarded incompetent evidence in reaching his verdict does not obtain where an objection to the evidence has been overruled. LOYOLA U L J 2:420, Summer, 1971.

Evidence—rape trials—victim's prior sexual history, by E. G. Johnson. BAYLOR L REV 27:362-369, Spring, 1975.

Examination of semen and saliva in a single stain, by L. O. Barsegiants. SUD MED EKSPERT 14:30-32, October-December, 1971.

Examining the sexual assault victim, by A. F. Schiff. J FL MED ASS 56:731-739, September 1969.

An experimental case study of the bio-feedback treatment of a rape-induced psychophysiological cardiovascular disorder, by E. B. Blanchard, et al. BEH THER 7(1):113-119, January, 1976.

Expertise in sex crimes, by R. Djordjic, et al. SRPSKI ARH CELOK LEK 97:159-166, February, 1969.

An exploratory study of five hundred sex offenders, by A. R. Pacht, et al. CRIM JUS BEH 1:13-20, March, 1974.

Exposure to erotic stimuli and sexual deviance, by M. J. Goldstein. J SOC ISSUES 29(3):197-219, 1973.

False accusations to camouflage autoerotic acts, by F. Kosa. ARCH KRIMINOL 148:106-110, September-October, 1971.

Felony, murder, rape and the mandatory death penalty: a study in discretionary justice, by H. A. Bedau. SUFFOLK U L REV 10:493-520, Spring, 1976.

Female child victims of sex offenses, by J. H. Gagnon. SOC PROB 13:176-192, Fall, 1965.

Female university student and staff perceptions of rape, by M. H. Herman, et al. J NATL ASSN WOMEN DEANS ADM & COUNSEL 38:20-23, Fall, 1974.

Feminists hold rape defense workshop, by G. Lichtenstein. N Y

TIMES 68, April 18, 1971.

Fight, by Erin. IT AIN'T ME BABE 1(10):14, July 23, 1970.

Fingerprints and criminal conviction, by K. Walker, et al. J COMM PSYCHOL 1(2):192-194, April, 1973.

The first half-hour, by L. Appell, et al. J PRACT NURS 26:16-18+, January, 1976.

For the rapist's victim, a place of sanctuary and sympathy, by B. Yoklavich. DAILY TELEGRAPH 17, May 23, 1975.

For victims of rape: many new types of help. U S NEWS 79: 44, December 8, 1975.

Forcible laceration of the rectum, by P. Altunkov, et al. KHIR-URGIIA 23:167-169, 1970.

Forcible rape, by M. Amir. FED PROBAT 31:51, March, 1967.

Forcible rape and problem of rights of accused, by E. Sagarin. INTELLECT 103(2366):515-520, 1975.

Forcible rape and the criminal justice system: surveying present practices and projecting future trends, by D. Chappell. CRIME & DELINQ 22:125-136, April, 1976.

Forcible rape: bibliography, by D. Chappell, et al. J CRIM LAW AND CRIM 65:248-263, June, 1974.

Forcible rape by multiple offenders, by G. Geis, et al. ABST ON CRIM & PENOL 11(4):431-436, 1971.

Four questions about sex in our society, by J. Kirk. MED TIMES 102(11):68-80, November, 1974.

Fraud in assault and rape, by A. Hooper. UBC L REV 3:117, May, 1968.

Free Wansley now. SOUTH PAT 32(1):1, January, 1974.

Freedom for rape frameup victim. BLACK PANTH 11(23):9, June 1, 1974.

The general opinion still is that anyone who has cheerful sex with a surplus of lovers cannot really be raped, by I. Kurtz. NOVA 9, October, 1975.

Genital injuries in childhood caused by rape, by J. Schafer, et al. ORV HETIL 113:2245-2246, September 10, 1972.

German drug better than jail. ADVOCATE 72:13, November 10, 1971.

Getting ripped off. EVERYWOMAN 1(14):13, February 5, 1971.

—. LADDER 15(3):23, December, 1970.

Giles vs Maryland. 87 Sup Ct 793. J URBAN L 46:118, 1968.

Girl's reputation: J. Roberts vs Giles brothers. TIME 86:44, August 6, 1965.

Good clean fun, by N. Drew. GREAT SPECKLED BIRD 3(44): 14, November 1, 1970.

Grady rape crisis center, by Krista. GREAT SPECKLED BIRD 7(26):13, July 1, 1974.

Group sexual assaults, by G. Geis. MED ASPECTS HUM SEXUAL 5(5):100-113, May, 1971.

Guidelines for the interview and examination of alleged rape victims: California Medical Association. WEST J MED 123:420-422, November, 1975.

Gynaecological findings in sexual offenses, by Sklovska. CESK GYNEKOL 40(10):721-723, December, 1975.

Harp/forever punished, by Harp. NORTHWEST PASS 11(6): 25, September 9, 1974.

Heads or tails: Women in American movies and society, a review of *From Reverence to Rape: the Treatment of Women in the Movies,* by M. Haskell. A review by D. J. Gorssvogel. DIA-CRIT 5(3):49-55, Fall, 1975.

Healthy rise in rape. NEWSWK 80:72, July 31, 1972.

Heilbron draws a veil. ECONOMIST 257:32-33, December 13, 1975.

Heilbron report, by J. C. Smith. CRIM L REV 97:106, February, 1976.

Help for rape victim, by B. S. Wallston. CRIM JUST BEH 3(1): 103-104, 1976.

Heroic rapist; excerpt from *Against Our Will: Men, Women and Rape,* by S. Brownmiller. MADEMOISELLE 81:128-129+, September, 1975.

High court backs naming of rape victims in news. ED & PUB 108:11+, March 8, 1975.

Hitching. ST LOUIS OUTLAW 2(12):20, December 3, 1971.

Hormone curbs sex offenders. AM DRUGGIST 159:53, May 5, 1969.

House-of-delegates redefines death, urges redefinition of rape, and undoes Houston amendments. ABA J 61:463-470, April, 1975.

How can a woman avoid rape? by E. Mason. INTELLECT 103: 512-513, May, 1975.

How much do you really know about rapists? excerpt from *Against Rape,* by A. Medea, et al. MS 3:113-114, July, 1974.

How rape is reported, by K. Soothill, et al. NEW SOC 702-704, June 19, 1975.

How to help raped, by J. Gilley. NEW SOC 28(612):756-758,

1974.

How to keep from being raped, by C. West. PROGRESS WO-MEN 2:16, April 2, 1972.

How to protect yourself from rape. GOOD H 181:157, September, 1975.

How to tell if your're being raped—and what to do about it; excerpt from *The Womansbook*, by V. Billings. REDBK 144: 70+, November, 1974.

How you can help the rape victim. NURSING '74 4:11, October, 1974.

The HRP Rape proposal, by Autin. HERSELF 3(2):12, May, 1974.

Hughes held for trial. ADVOCATE 35:12, April 10, 1974.

I should have known: it's August, by C. Heimel. MAJ REP 4:1+, August 22, 1974.

If she consented once, she consented again—a legal fallacy in forcible rape cases. VAL U L REV 10:127-167, Fall, 1975.

I'll tell you what it's like in jail, by Johnston. GAY 2(64):4, November 22, 1971.

Illinois hospitals required to give rape victims free care. HOSP 49:17, September 16, 1975.

Immunological method of establishing the presence and species of seminal stains, by V. P. Chernov. SUD MED EKSPERT 14:28-30, October-December, 1971.

Imposition of the death penalty for rape where the victim's life has been neither taken nor endangered constitutes cruel and unusual punishment under the eighth amendment. HOUS-TON L REV 8:795, March, 1971.

In defense of Sis Joanne: for ourselves and history, by M. R.

Karenga. BLACK SCHOLAR 6:37-42, July, 1975.

Incidence of the death penalty for rape in Virginia, by D. H. Partington. WASH & LEE L REV 22:43, Spring, 1965.

Indecent assaults on minor girls. Data concerning individuals and environment, by K. G. Stukat. SOCIALMED T 41:437-443, December, 1964.

Indiana's rape shield law: conflict with the confrontation clause? IND L REV 9:418-440, January, 1976.

Indicia of consent? LOYOLA U L J 7:118-140, Winter, 1976.

Indignities and perversions. GAY LIBERATOR 34:7, February, 1974.

Inez Garcia on trial, by N. Blitman, et al. MS 3:49-54+, May, 1975.

Injuries during coitus, by M. Chomakov, et al. AKUSH GINEK 4:223-227, 1965.

Intelligent woman's guide to sex: social rape, by K. Durbin. MADEMOISELLE 81:58, September, 1975.

Interagency service network to meet needs of rape victims, by G. Hardgrove. SOC CASE 57(4):245-253, 1976.

An investigation of the responses of convicted rapists to erotic stimuli, by G. A. Kercher. DISS ABST INTERNATL 32 (1-B):541-542, July, 1971.

Is rape a sex crime? by D. Ben-Horin. NATION 221:112-115, August 16, 1975.

Is rape what women really want? by C. Calvert. MADEMOIS-ELLE 78:134-135+, March, 1974.

It is always the woman who is raped, by D. Metzger. AM J PSYCH 133:405-408, April, 1976.

Jack A.—How rape is reported, by K. Soothill. NEW SOC 32 (663):702-704, 1975.

Jack A. Gibbens TCN-Rape—22-year cohort study, by K. L. Soothill. MED SCI LAW 16(1):62-69, 1976.

Jack the raper. W BRIDGE 3(41):18, October 9, 1970.

—. IT AIN'T ME BABE 1(13):5, September 4, 1970.

Jail is like another world, by B. Calvert. WIN 6(14):11, September 1, 1970.

Jenkins consents. ECONOMIST 225:19, June 21, 1975.

Joanne Little: America goes on trial. FREEDOMWAYS 15(2): 87-88, August, 1975.

JoAnne Little: the dialectics of rape, by A. Davis. MS 3:74-77+, June, 1975.

Judge and jury attitudes to rape, by R. Barber. AUSTRALIAN & NEW ZEALAND J OF CRIM 7:157-172, September, 1974.

Judge rescinds order to close rape hearing. ED & PUB 108:33, July 5, 1975.

Judicial attitudes toward rape victims, by C. Bohmer. JUDICATURE 57:303-307, February, 1974.

Justice for Franca; challenging Mafia traditions by prosecuting her abductor in Sicily. NEWSWK 69:37, January 2, 1967.

Kick-ass for women. OLD MOLE 1(45):6, August 7, 1970.

Lasting psychotic regression in a 4-year-old girl, victim of a rape, by C. Koupernik. REV NEUROPSYCHIAT INFANT SUPPL 63:66, 1967.

Law enforcement's participation in crisis counseling for rape victims, by J. Stratton. POLICE CHIEF 43(3):46-49, 1976.

30

The law of rape, by F. H. A. Micklewright. LABOUR MO 57: 314-317, July, 1975.

The law on rape, by M. Colton. WOMEN SPEAKING 4(7), July-September, 1975.

Least punished crime. NEWSWK 80:33, December 18, 1972.

A letter to Michele, by Suter. WIN 7(14):22, September 15, 1971.

Liability to punishment for pregnancy interruptions following rape, in the new penal code? by H. J. Rieger. DEUTSCH MED WSCHR 94:507, March 7, 1969.

Like Ann's gynecologist or time I was almost raped—personal narratives in women's rap groups, by S. Kalcik. J AM FOLKLO 88(347):3-11, 1975.

Limitations on the right to introduce evidence pertaining to the prior sexual history of the complaining witness in cases of forcible rape: reflection of reality or denial of due process? HOFSTRA L REV 3:403-426, Spring, 1975.

Long Island woman gang raped. GAY 2(58):12, August 30, 1971.

Lucky death sentence; retrial of Giles brothers. TIME 90:81, November 10, 1967.

Males may claim rape under Massachusetts law. ADVOCATE 46:12, Setpember 11, 1974.

Management of sexually assaulted females, by J. B. Massey, et al. OBSTET GYNECOL 38:29-36, July, 1971.

Medical aspects of rape, by A. Frank, et al. MADEMOISELLE 82:46-47, February, 1976.

Medical assessment of the sexually assaulted female, by C. A. Ringrose. MED TRIAL TECHN QUART 15:59-61, December, 1968.

Medical care for the sexually assaulted, by J. H. Davis. J FL
MED ASS 61:588, July, 1974.

Medical examination in sexual offenses, by D. M. Paul. MED
SCI & L 15:154-162, July, 1975.

The medical examination of cases of rape, by W. F. Enos, et al.
J FORENSIC SCI 17(1):50-56, January, 1972.

Medical investigation of alleged rape, by I. Root, et al. WEST J
MED 120:329-333, April, 1974.

Medico-legal considerations on the presence of a tampax in the
vaginal orifice during a rape, by P. L'Epee, et al. MED LEG
DOMM CORPOR 1:180-181, April, 1968.

Medicolegal examination of the hymen, by A. Debarge, et al.
MED LEG DOMM CORPOR 6:298-300, July-September,
1973.

The mental health committee: report of the Subcommittee on
the problem of rape in the District of Columbia, by E. H.
Weiss, et al. MED ANN DC 41:703-704, November, 1972.

Michigan's criminal sexual assault law, by K. A. Cobb, et al. U
MICH J L REF 8:217-236, Fall, 1974.

Mississippi justice; white man's life imprisonment. NEWSWK
66:42, November 22, 1965.

Missouri justices red faced. ADVOCATE 70:19, October 13,
1971.

The modification of sexual fantasies: a combined treatment approach to the reduction of deviant sexual behavior, by W. L.
Marshall. BEH RES & THER 11(4):557-564, November,
1973.

Modification of the Berg acid phosphatase test, by A. F. Schiff.
J FORENSIC SCI 14:538-544, October, 1969.

The molested young female. Evaluation and therapy of alleged

32

rape, by J. L. Breen, et al. PEDIATR CLIN NORTH AM 19:717-725, August, 1972.

Motive for murder. ECONOMIST 255:71, April 12, 1975.

Murder. ST LOUIS OUTLAW 1(13):2, March 5, 1971.

My fourteen years on death row, by E. Labat, et al. LOOK 32: 80+, March 19, 1968.

My husband was accused of rape: case of mistaken identity. GOOD H 178:16+, April, 1974.

NAWL/IBA program—rapporteur's report, by L. Penland, et al. WOMEN LAW J 60:176-207, Fall, 1974.

Natural law and unnatural acts, by J. M. Finnis. HEYTHROP J 11:365-387, October, 1970.

Nature and quality of the act: a re-evaluation. OTTAWA L REV 3:340, Fall, 1968.

Nebraska's corroboration rule. NEB L REV 54:93-110, 1975.

New drug curbs sex urge, by Larsson. GAY 2(63):10, November 8, 1971.

The new Florida rape law, by A. F. Schiff. J FL MED ASS 62(9):40-42, September, 1975.

New rights for rape victims, by A. A. Sant. MAJ REP 4:9, February 8, 1975.

New York women discuss rape, by Hardy. MILITANT 35(17): 17, May 7, 1971.

Nice girls don't get into trouble, by G. Sheehy. N Y MAG February 15, 1971.

Nice girls don't get raped, do they? by E. Paris. CHATELAINE 44:31, 70-72+, September, 1971.

Nidation inhibition and abortion following rape, by E. Bohm, et al. MED KLIN 66:989-996, July 2, 1971.

Night of rape and death in jail. ADVOCATE 40:12, June 19, 1974.

Nocturnal penile tumescence and sleep of convicted rapists and other prisoners, by I. Karacan, et al. ARCH OF SEX BEH 3(1):19-26, January, 1974.

Nonviolent self defense, by Morris. WIN 10(2):8, January 24, 1974.

Normal, healthy and pleasurable, by R. Moody. PEACE NEWS 17(95):6, November 20, 1970.

A note on stress and sex determination by I. Wittles, et al. J GEN PSYCHOL 124(2):333-334, June, 1974.

Note to southern women, by Paula. GREAT SPECKLED BIRD 7(10):3, March 11, 1974.

Nursing coverage: patient raped by orderly. REGAN REP NURS L 16:2, February, 1976.

The offense of rape in Victoria, by E. J. Hodgens, et al. AUSTRALIAN & NEW ZEALAND J OF CRIM 5(4):225-240, 1972.

Ohio's new rape law: does it protect complainant at the expense of the rights of the accused? AKRON L REV 9:337-359, Fall, 1975.

On black women, by A. Davis. MS 1:55+, August, 1972.

On rape, by D. Densmore. NO MORE FUN AND GAMES 6: 57-84, May, 1973.

On the castration of sexual assailants detained according to paragraph 42b of the German Penal Code, by H. W. Muller, et al. NERVENARZT 39:360-365, August, 1968.

—. Late recurrences, sterilization of criminals detained according to paragraph 42b of the German Penal Code, by A. Langeluddeke. NERVENARZT 39:265-268, August, 1968.

On the use of a particular technic to make a more precise diagnosis of hymenal integrity, by G. Dellepiana. MINERVA MEDICOLEG 84:37-43, May-June, 1964.

One reading of rape, by C. Macinnes. NEW SOC 33(667):147, July 17, 1975.

The oral rape fantasy and rejection of mother in the imagery of Shakespear's Venus and Adonis, by A. B. Rothenberg. PSYCHOANAL Q 40:447-468, 1971.

Organizing a rape crisis program in a general hospital, by E. Bassuk, et al. J AM MED WOM ASSOC 30(12):486-490, December, 1975.

Other crimes evidence to prove intent in rape cases. LOYOLA L REV 19:751-758, Fall, 1973.

Our sisters speak. Rape: the response. WOMEN: A J OF LIB 3:2.

The pattern of rape in Singapore, by A. Y. Ng. SINGAPORE MED J 15:49-50, March, 1974.

Patterns in forcible rape, by M. Amir. A review by A. J. Reiss, et al. AM J SOC 80(3):785, 1974.

—. A review by R. Lotz. CONT SOC 4(4):381-382, 1975.

Patterns in forcible rape: a review-essay. CRIM L BULL 9:703-710, October, 1973.

Patterns of response among victims of rape, by S. Sutherland, et al. AM J ORTHOP 40:503-511, April, 1970.

People vs English. 209 N E 2d 722. BROOK L REV 32:434, April, 1966.

People vs Hernandez. 393 P 2d 673.

—in ALA L REV 17:101, Fall, 1964.
    AM CRIM L Q 4:57, Fall, 1965.
    ARIZ L REV 7:324, Spring, 1966.
    CATHOLIC U L REV 14:123, January, 1965.
    DE PAUL L REV 14:449, Spring-Summer, 1965.
    DENVER L J 41:322, September-October, 1964.
    GA SB J 1:552, May, 1965.
    GEO L J 53:506, Winter, 1965.
    GEO WASH L REV 33:588, December, 1964.
    HARV L REV 78:1257, April, 1965.
    HASTINGS L J 16:270, November, 1964.
    IA L REV 50:628, Winter, 1965.
    J FAMILY L 5:107, Spring, 1965.
    MINN L REV 50:170, November, 1965.
    MISS LAW J 36:254, March, 1965.
    MONTANA L REV 26:133, Fall, 1964.
    NC L REV 43:424, February, 1965.
    ND L REV 41:59, November, 1964.
    ORE L REV 44:243, April, 1965.
    SO CALIF L REV 38:131, 1965.
    STAN L REV 17:309, January, 1965.
    SYRACUSE L REV 16:148, Fall, 1964.
    U COLO L REV 37:295, Winter, 1965.
    UMKC L REV 33:158, Winter, 1965.
    VAND L REV 18:244, December, 1964.
    W VA L REV 67:149, February, 1965.
    WASH & LEE L REV 22:119, Spring, 1965.
    WASHBURN L J 5:141, Winter, 1965.
    WAYNE L REV 11:556, Winter, 1965.

People vs Lombardi. 229 N E 2d 206. ST JOHN'S L REV 42: 604, April, 1968.

People vs Rincon-Pineda, rape trials depart the seventeenth century—farewell to Lord Hale. TULSA L J 11:279-290, 1975.

Personality characteristics of rapists, by W. C. Perdue, et al. PERCEP & MOTOR SKILLS 35(2):514, October, 1972.

Physical evidence in rape cases, by L. R. Vitallo. J POLIC SCI

2(2):160, 1974.

Pig charged. SEC CITY 2(10):4, October, 1970.

Pig exonerated. SEC CITY 2(11):2, November, 1970.

Planning a rape conference, by Kellogg. RAT 20:10, March 2, 1971.

Police discretion and the judgment that a crime has been committed—rape in Philadelphia. U PA LAW R 117:277, December, 1968.

Police processing of rape complaints: a case study. AM J CRIM L 4:15-30, Winter, 1975-1976.

Political prisoners/Carrington. WORK WORLD 16(16):19, August 26, 1974.

The politics of rape—a selective history, by R. Lacks. VILLAGE VOICE February 4, 1971.

Portrait of a rapist. NEWSWK 82:67, August 20, 1973.

Postcoital estrogens in cases of rape, by M. G. Chapman. NEW ENG J MED 280:277, January 30, 1969.

Pride of Inez Garcia, by M. Del Drago. MS 3:54+, May, 1975.

Primitive crimes under the aspects of the evolutional layer therapy and animal behavior research, by K. Jarosch. WIEN KLIN WSCHR 77:757-760, October 15, 1965.

The professional as a court witness, by A. W. Burgess, et al. J EMERGENCY NURS 2:25-30, March-April, 1976.

Proposed amendments to the criminal code with respect to the victims of rape and related sexual offenses, by G. R. Goodman. MAN L J 6:275-281, 1975.

Psychiatric and legal aspects of statutory rape, pregnancy and abortion in juveniles, by M. Shopper. J PSYCH & L 1(3):

275-295, Fall, 1973.

The psychic effects of criminal assaults in chidlhood, by E. Nau. DEUTSCH Z GES GERICHTL MED 55:172-173, September 1, 1964.

Psychodynamics of pornography, by K. S. Walshe-Brennan. NURS MIRROR 142:58-60, January 1, 1976.

Psychogenic retention of urine, by L. Aubert, et al. J UROL NEPHROL 74:903-905, October-November, 1968.

Psychological needs of rapists, by G. Fisher, et al. BRIT J CRIM 11:182-185, April, 1971.

Psychology constructs the female; or the fantasy life of the male psychologist (with some attention to the fantasies of his friends, the male biologist and the male anthropologist), by N. Weisstein. SOC ED 35(4):362-373, April, 1971.

The psychology of rapists, by M. L. Cohen, et al. SEMIN PSYCH 3(3):307-327, August, 1971.

Psychosoziale Aspeke von Sexualdelikten an Kindern, by H. Prahm. MSCHR KRIMIN & STRAFRECHTSREFORM 57:193-198, August, 1974.

A public health program for sexually assaulted females, by C. R. Hayman, et al. PUB HEALTH REP. 82:497-504, June, 1967.

The public image of the sex offender, by G. J. Falk. MENT HYG 48:612-620, October, 1964.

Putting the sex back into rape, by T. Branch. WASH M 8:56-62, March, 1976.

Q. If you rape a woman and steal her TV, what can they get you for in New York? by M. W. Lear. N Y TIMES MAG 10-11+, January 30, 1972; Discussion p. 24+, February 27, 1972.

Quick woman foils the pig. BERKELEY TRIBE 72:2, November 20, 1970.

Race, judicial discretion and the death penalty, by M. Wolfgang, et al. ANN AM ACAD POLITIC & SOC SCI 407:119-133, May, 1973.

Racist use of rape charge, by Hardin. SOUTH PAT 32(7):3, September, 1974.

Racist use of rape charge, by Golos. WORK WORLD 16(10):11, May 17, 1974.

Racist use of rape laws, by Smith. MILITANT 38(24):12, June 21, 1974.

Rape. EVERYWOMAN 1(14):8, February 5, 1971.

Rape. MEDICOLEG J 44(1):1-5, 1976.

Rape, by G. Sheridan, et al. GUARDIAN 11, January 15, 1975.

Rape, by J. Selkin. PSYCHOL TODAY 8:70-72+, January, 1975.

Rape. GAY LIBERATOR 39:1, August, 1974.

Rape. NORTHWEST PASS 11(4):24, July 29, 1974.

Rape. OTHER WOMAN 2(5):12, June, 1974.

Rape. OTHER WOMAN 2(6):2, July, 1974.

Rape, by R. Hartman. ILL MED J 145:518-519, June, 1974.

Rape. HARRY 2(18):9, August 16, 1971.

Rape. FIFTH ESTATE 5(24):17, April 1, 1971.

Rape. NOLA EXPR 1(55):3, May 15, 1970.

Rape: a complex management problem in the pediatric emergency room, by G. L. Lipton, et al. J PEDIAT 75:859-866,

November, 1969.

Rape: a compulsion to destroy, by W. Brombert, et al. MED IN-SIGHT 6:20-22, April, 1974.

Rape: a normal act? by R. G. Kasinsky. CAN FORUM 55:18-22, September, 1975.

Rape: a plea for help in the hospital emergency room, by C. C. Williams, et al. NURS FORUM 12:388-401, 1973.

Rape: a 22-year cohort study, by K. L. Soothill, et al. MED SCI LAW 16(1):62-69, January, 1976.

Rape after the rape. HERSELF 3(2):13, May, 1974.

Rape after the rape. GAY LIBERATOR 34:6, February, 1974.

Rape alert, by J. K. Footlick, et al. NEWSWK 86:70-72+, November 10, 1975.

Rape, an analysis, by Nett. WOMENS PRESS 1(6):10, July, 1971.

Rape—an ugly movie trend, by A. Harmetz. N Y TIMES, ARTS & LEIS September 30, 1973.

Rape and consent. TIME 105:55, May 12, 1975.

Rape and death penalty. PEACEMAK 27(6):2, May 4, 1974.

Rape and nursing intervention: locating resources, by S. Louie. IMPRINT 22:27+, December, 1975.

Rape and other sexual offenses, by J. Barnes. BRIT MED J 2: 293-295, April 29, 1967.

Rape and police protection, by Hutchinson. GREAT SPECK-LED BIRD 4(42):5, October 18, 1971.

Rape and rape laws: sexism in society and law, by C. E. Le-Grand. CALIF L REV 61:919-941, May, 1973.

Rape and self defense. GREAT SPECKLED BIRD 7(11):12, March 18, 1974.

Rape and self defense. SEED 7(11):31, November, 1971.

Rape and social structure, by D. Lester. PSYCHOL REP 35(1): 146, 1974.

Rape and the fallen woman, by Griffin. EVERYWOMAN 2(15): 1, October 26, 1971.

Rape and the Harlem women: she asked for it—or did she? by M. Walker. MAJ REP 4:1+, August 22, 1974.

Rape and the law in the United States: an historical and socio- logical analysis, by E. C. Viano. INTERNATL J CRIM & PENOL 2:317-328, November, 1974.

Rape and the trauma of inadequate care, by M. S. Welch. PRISM 3:17+, September, 1975.

Rape and what to do about it, by J. Kole. HARP BAZ 109:118- 119+, March, 1976.

Rape as a capital offense in 19th century Queensland, by R. Barber. AUST J POL 21(1):31-41, 1975.

Rape as a heinous but understudied offense, by N. S. Goldner. J CRIM LAW AND CRIM 63:402, September, 1972.

Rape—attitudinal training for police and emergency room person- nel, by M. L. Keefe, et al. POLICE CHIEF 42(11):36-37, 1975.

Rape/be strong, fight back. AUGUR 2(16):3, June, 1971.

Rape: breaking the silence; with the rising tide of sexual assaults women have organized crisis centers to assist the victims, by M. Wasserman. PROGRESS 37:19-23, November, 1973.

Rape case that shook Maryland: Giles case, by T. W. Lippman. REPORT 38:32-34, March 7, 1968.

Rape corroboration requirement: repeal not reform. YALE L J 81:1365, June, 1972.

Rape/crime of violence, by Krista. GREAT SPECKLED BIRD 7(10):3, March 11, 1974.

Rape crisis line. GIDRA 6(2):3, February, 1974.

Rape/last prosecuted violent crime, by Griffin. WOMENS PRESS 1(9):10, October, 1971.

Rape: exploding the myths, by E. Bernstein, et al. TODAYS HEALTH 53:36-39+, October, 1975.

Rape fantasies, by S. H. Kardener. J REL & HEALTH 14(1): 50-57, January, 1975.

Rape: hospitals can do more than treat the victim, by H. Freilich. HOSP MED STAFF 4:1-7, September, 1975.

Rape in foreign countries, by A. F. Schiff. MED TRIAL TECHN QUART 20:66-74, Summer, 1973.

—, by A. F. Schiff. MED TRIAL TECHN QUART Annual 66-74, 1974.

Rape in Illinois: a denial of equal protection. JOHN MARSHAL J 8:457-496, Spring, 1975.

Rape in literature, by C. A. Douglas. THE SEC WAVE 2:2.

Rape in other countries, by A. F. Schiff. MED SCI LAW 11(3): 139-143, 1971.

Rape in prison, by A. M. Scacco. A review by H. E. Allen. J CRIM JUS 3(4):333-334, 1975.

Rape in the District of Columbia, by C. R. Hayman, et al. AM J OBSTET GYNECOL 113:91-97, May 1, 1972.

Rape: interruption of the therapeutic process by external stress, by A. Werner. PSYCHOTHERAPY: THEORY RES &

PRAC 9(4):349-351, Winter, 1972.

Rape is a four-letter word, by M. R. Schulz. ETC 32:65-69, March, 1975.

Rape is an ugly word. EMER MED 3:23-27, October, 1971.

Rape law, by Liddell. WOMENS PRESS 1(7):3, August, 1971.

Rape law in Texas: H. B. 284 and the road to reform, by S. Weddington. AM J CRIM L 4:1-14, Winter, 1975-1976.

Rape law revised. GAY LIB 39:3, August, 1974.

Rape law: the need for reform, by R. B. Washburn. NEW MEX L REV 5:279-309, May, 1975.

Rape: most rapidly increasing crime, by R. Koenig. MC CALLS 100:25, July, 1973.

Rape myths: in legal, theoretical, and everyday practice, by J. R. Schwendinger, et al. CRIME AND SOC JUS 1:18-26, Spring-Summer, 1974.

Rape needs a special examination, by A. F. Schiff. EMER MED 3:28-29, October, 1971.

Rape: no woman is immune, by C. See. TODAYS HEALTH 53:30, October 5, 1975.

The rape of Sheila Robinson, by R. Bruce. IMPRINT 22:32-33+, December, 1975.

Rape-offenders and their victims, by J. M. Macdonald. A review by B. Greenspan. FAM COORD 22:257, 1973.

Rape or suspected rape cases. J LOUISIANA MED SOC 119:319-320, August, 1967.

Rape prevention tactics. MS 3:114-115, July, 1974.

Rape, race and the death penalty in Georgia, by M. E. Wolfgang, et al. AM J ORTHOP 45:658-668, July, 1975.

Rape reality, rape fantasy; discussion, by P. Steinfels. COMMONWEAL 102:554+, November 21, 1975.

—. COMMONWEAL 103:59-61+, January 16, 1976.

Rape reform legislation: is it the solution? CLEV ST L R 24: 463-503, 1975.

Rape, seduction and love-ethics in public and private communication, by C. H. Harpole. SPEECH TEAC 24(4):303-308, 1975.

Rape squad; Manhattan sex crimes squad, by G. Lichtenstein. N Y TIMES MAG 10-11+, March 3, 1974.

Rape: the all-American crime, by S. Griffin. RAMP 10:26-35, September, 1971.

Rape: the double standard, by L. Kuby. APHRA 5:31-35, Winter, 1973-1974.

Rape/the experience. ST LOUIS OUTLAW 1(14):4, March 24, 1971.

Rape: the man-made myth, by S. Griffin. NOVA 68-71, December, 1971.

Rape: the medical, social, and legal implications, by J. R. Evrard. AM J OBSTET GYNECOL 111:197-199, September 15, 1971.

Rape: the ultimate violation of the self, by E. Hilberman. AM J PSYCH 133:436-437, April, 1976.

Rape—the ultimate invasion of privacy, by L. C. Cottell. FBI L ENFORCE BULL 43(5):2-6, 1974.

Rape: the unmentionable crime, by A. Lake. GOOD H 173: 104-105+, November, 1971.

Rape: the victim and the criminal justice system, by L. L. Holmstrom, et al. INTERNATL J CRIM & PENOL 3:101-110, May, 1975.

Rape: the victim as defendant, by S. Landau. TRIAL 10:19+, July-August, 1974.

Rape trauma syndrome, by A. W. Burgess, et al. AM J PSYCH 131(9):981-986, September, 1974.

—. NURS DIGEST 3:17-19, May-June, 1975.

Rape treatment centers set up in two cities. J AM MED ASS 233:11+, July 7, 1975.

Rape victim: a victim of society and the law. WILLAMETTE L J 11:36-55, Winter, 1974.

The rape victim and due process, by A. Blumberg. CASE AND COM 80:3-17, November-December, 1975.

Rape victim counseling: the legal process; adapted from *Rape: Victims of Crisis,* by A. W. Burgess, et al. J NATL ASSN WOMEN DEANS ADM & COUNSEL 38:24-31, Fall, 1974.

Rape victim defends slaying, by Seneche. NORTHWEST PASS 11(7):26, September 23, 1974.

—. NEW TIMES 6(4):5, September 11, 1974.

Rape victim guidelines. MOD HEALTH CARE 3(3):74, March, 1975.

Rape victim in the emergency ward, by A. W. Burgess, et al. AM J NURSING 73:1740-1745, October, 1973.

The rape victim: is she also the unintended victim of the law? by A. Taylor. N Y TIMES June 15, 1971.

Rape victim: psychodynamic considerations, by M. T. Notman, et al. AM J PSYCH 133:408-413, April, 1976.

Rape victimology, by L. G. Schultz. A review by H. G. Beigel. J SEX RES 12(1):74, 1975.

—. A review by A. J. Davis. AM J PSYCH 132(12):1341-1342.

—. A review by L. L. Holmstrom. SEX ROLES 1(4):398-400, 1975.

—. A review by A. K. Mant. MED SCI LAW 16(1):76, 1976.

—. A review by F. R. Scarpitti. J MARRIAGE 37(4):1038-1040, 1975.

Rape—victims of crisis, by A. W. Burgess, et al. A review. AM J PSYCH 132(4):462-463.

Rape victim's picture and name front paged, by C. M. Rupp. ED & PUB 108:8, May 31, 1975.

Rape victims: reasons, responses and reforms, by P. A. Hartwig, et al. INTELLECT 103:507-511, May, 1975.

Rape victims tell libbers what it's like, by M. McNellis. N Y SUNDAY NEWS 36, April 18, 1971.

Rape victims—the invisible patients, by V. Price. CAN NURSE 71(4):29-34, April, 1975.

Rape victims: the unpopular patients, by E. LeBourdais. DI-MEN HEALTH SERV 53:12-14, March, 1976.

Rape: violating the other man's property, by J. Thompson. BROADSHEET: NEW ZEALAND'S FEM MAG 33:30-33, October, 1975.

Rape wave; creation of rape investigation and analysis section. NEWSWK 81:59, January 29, 1973.

Rape: when to fight back, by J. Selkin. PSYCHOL TODAY 8: 70-72+, January, 1975.

Rape/whom does the law protect, by Mastalli. COLL PRESS

SER 45:4, March 20, 1974.

Raped. RISING UP ANGRY 2(5):5, January, 1971.

Raped women of Bangladesh, by B. Karkaria. ILL WEEKLY OF INDIA 93:14-17, June 18, 1972.

Rapists assailed/anti-rapist deman. BERKELEY TRIBE 71:12, November 13, 1970.

Rapists, molesters got less porn. ADVOCATE 50:5, January 6, 1971.

Rashomon in Maryland: Giles-Johnson rape case, by S. Brownmiller. ESQUIRE 69:130-132+, May, 1968.

Reactions of convicted rapists to sexually explicit stimuli, by G. A. Kercher, et al. J ABNORM PSYCHOL 81(1):46-50, February, 1973.

Real spoils of war; excerpt from *Against Our Will: Men, Women and Rape,* by S. Brownmiller. MS 4:82-85, December, 1975.

Reasonable mistake as to age—a defense to statutory rape under the new penal code. CONN L REV 2:433, Winter, 1969-1970.

Reasonable mistake of age: a needed defense to statutory rape, by L. W. Myers. MICH L REV 64:105, November, 1965.

Reasonable rape: statutory rape. TIME 87:49, January 21, 1966.

A reasoned approach to the reform of sex offense legislation, by R. B. Schram. PROSPECTUS 1:139-161, April, 1968.

Recent statutory developments in the definition of forcible rape. VA L REV 61:1500-1543, November, 1975.

Regina vs Schell. No. 88 of 1964, Law Society Reports, Tas. TASMANIAN U L REV 2:202, November 1965.

Report to the Hague: suggested revisions of penal laws relating to sex crimes and crimes against the family, by M. Ploscowe. CORNELL LAW Q 50:425-445, Spring, 1965.

Requem et Caveat, by St. John. EVERYWOMAN 1(12):3, January, 1971.

Requirements of corroboration in rape cases repealed, by M. Weinstein. QUEEN'S BAR BULL 38:23-28, October, 1974.

Resistance standard in rape legislation. STAN L REV 18:680, February, 1966.

Return of the phantom; arrest of M. Brookins. NEWSWK 74: 24, July 14, 1969.

Reverence to Rape—Treatment of Women in Movies, by M. Haskell, et al. A review. NATION 220(6):182-184, 1975.

Review of child molestation and alleged rape cases, by H. A. Robinson, Jr., et al. AM J OBSTET GYNECOL 110:405-406, June 1, 1971.

Revolt against rape. TIME 104:85, July 22, 1974.

Revolt against rape; with views of S. Brownmiller. TIME 106: 48+, October 13, 1975.

Right to privacy; overturning of a Georgia statute forbidding publication of a rape victim's name, by J. K. Footlick, et al. NEWSWK 85:66, March 17, 1975.

Rise in rape spurs action, by Krista. GREAT SPECKLED BIRD 7(19):5, May 13, 1974.

The role of the victim in sex offenses, by A. Menachem, et al, in SEXUAL BEHAVIORS: SOCIAL CLINICAL AND LEGAL ASPECTS, edited by H. L. Resnik, et al. Boston: Little, Brown, 1972.

Roots and branches, by Hutton, et al. ANN ARBOR SUN 2(14):14, July 14, 1974.

Rx for rape the listening ear. EMER MED 7:240-243+, February, 1975.

Safety in the home, by Price, et al. MAJ REP 4(7):2, July 25, 1974.

St. Louis trains policewomen/rape squad. FOCUS—MIDWEST 9(60):6, nd.

Self-confidence/self-defense, by S. Cordell. THE SEC WAVE 2:4.

Self defense. GAY LIBERATOR 34:6, February, 1974.

Self-defense against rape: the Joanne Little case, by J. Bond. BLACK SCHOLAR 6:29-31, March, 1975.

Self defense class. WOMENS PRESS 4(1):17, February, 1974.

Self defense, preserve of females, by J. Lafferty. J FEM LIB 4:96, April, 1970.

The series rapist Bernhard N. Report on a murderer released from prison, by G. Bauer. ARCH KRIMINOL 147:65-73, March-April, 1971.

Serological tests for syphillis in rape cases. J AM MED ASS 228:1227-1228, June 3, 1974.

—, by M. I. Greenberg. J AM MED ASS 227:1381, March 25, 1974.

Seven who were raped, by B. Donadio, et al. NURS OUTLOOK 22:245-247, April, 1974.

Sex & the law: some officials invoke ancient sex statutes—selectively, critics say, by S. N. Sesser. WALL ST J 172:1, July 5, 1968.

Sex books and rape: FBI chief sees close links, by J. E. Hoover. U S NEWS 64:14-15, March 11, 1968.

Sex-crime and its socio-historical background, by F. E. Frenkel. J HIST IDEAS 25:333-352, July, 1964.

Sex crimes committed against children, by W. Becker. MED KLIN 59:1597-1601, October 2, 1964.

Sex crimes I should have known, by Heimel. MAJ REP 4(9):1, August 22, 1974.

Sex-'n-'violence, by B. Brophy. NEW STATESM 69:677-678, April 30, 1965.

Sex offenses and sex offenders, by D. E. J. MacNamara. ANN AM ACAD POLITIC & SOC SCI 376:148-155, March, 1968.

The sex offenses of blacks and whites, by S. A. Kirk. ARCH OF SEX BEH 4(3):295-302, May, 1975.

Sexual assault bill, by Rzepka. HERSELF 3(2):13, May, 1974.

Sexual assault center: Harborview Medical Center, Seattle. HOSP 48:22, June 1, 1974.

Sexual assault of female children, by V. J. Capraro. ANN NY ACAD SCI 142:817-819, May 10, 1967.

Sexual assault on women and children in the District of Columbia, by C. R. Hayman, et al. PUB HEALTH REP 83:1021-1028, December, 1968.

Sexual assault on women and girls, by C. R. Hayman, et al. AM J OBSTET GYNECOL 109:480-486, February 1, 1971.

Sexual assault on women and girls in the District of Columbia, by C. R. Hayman, et al. SOUTH MED J 62:1227-1231, October, 1969.

Sexual assault package: a refinement of a previous idea, by P. M. Fahrney. J AM COLL EMERGENCY PHYSICIANS 4:340-341, July-August, 1975.

Sexual assault program: District of Columbia, by R. L. Standard.

MED ANN DC 41:95-96, February, 1972.

Sexual assault: signs and symptoms, by A. W. Burgess, et al. J EMERGENCY NURSING 1:10-15, March-April, 1975.

Sexual assaults on children, by J. McGeorge. MED SCI LAW 4:245-253, October, 1964.

Sexual assaults on women and girls, by C. R. Hayman. ANN INTERN MED 72:277-278, February, 1970.

Sexual crimes and the medical examiner: interview with Milton Helpern. MED ASPECTS HUM SEXUAL 8(4):161-168, April, 1974.

Sexual criminality in the early Renaissance: Venice 1338-1358, by G. Ruggiero. J SOC HIST 8:18-37, Summer, 1975.

Sexual liberation and the adolescent girl, by F. Lieberman. BIRTH FAM J 2:51-56, Spring, 1975.

Sexual molestations in hospitals. The role of the physician and other suggestions of management, by R. Cohen. CLIN PEDIAT 3:689-691, December, 1964.

Sexual offenses act, by Arran. ENCOUNTER 38:3-8, March, 1972.

Sexualstraftater, by E. Schorsch. ENKE 230-249, 1971.

Simple question of rape, by S. Alexander. NEWSWK 84:110, October 28, 1974.

Singles rapist makes the daily news. MAJ REP 4(7):3, July 25, 1974.

Sisterhood strikes again, by A. Leffler. AIN'T I A WOMAN 3:5.

Sisters pick up sister. EVERYWOMAN 1(14):8, February, 1971.

Sisters sister/defense against rape, by Kelly. ANN ARBOR SUN

21:9, November 26, 1971.

Slight case of rape, by G. Robertson. NEW STATESM 89: 614+, May 9, 1975.

A slight case of rape, by A. Watkins. SPECTATOR 225, August 20, 1965.

Social and cultural determinants of the aggressive behavior of the participants in gange rapes, by C. Czapow. PRZEGLAD PENITENCJARNY I KRYMINOLOGICZNY 11(1):3-17, 1973.

Social, legal, and psychological effects of rape on the victim, by J. J. Peters. PA MED 78(2):34-36, February, 1975.

Society blamed for sexual assaults, by M. Goldstein. NEWSDAY 15A, April 19, 1971.

Sociological, medical and legal aspects of rape, by C. A. Ringrose. CRIM L Q 17(4):440-445, 1975.

Sociology: A Biographical Approach, by P. L. Berger, et al. A review by U. Planck. SOCIOL RUR 15(3):208-209, 1975.

Some psychological aspects of seduction, incest and rape in childhood, by M. Lewis, et al. J AM ACAD CHILD PSYCH 8:606-619, October, 1969.

Some reflections on sexual relations between physicians and patients, by B. Van Emde. J SEX RES 1966.

Special cases: rape victims' plight gets wide attention from police, courts, by J. C. Simpson. WALL ST J 186:1+, July 14, 1975.

Sperm identification-acid phosphatase test, by A. F. Schiff. MED TRIAL TECHN QUART 21(4):467-474, Spring, 1975.

Standard rape investigation form, by W. F. Enos, et al. VA MED MON 101:43-44, January, 1974.

A statistical evaluation of rape, by A. F. Schiff. J FORENSIC SCI 2:339-349, August, 1973.

Statistical features of rape, by A. F. Schiff. J FORENSIC SCI 14:102-110, January, 1969.

Statutory rape: a critique. LA L REV 26:105, December, 1965.

Statutory rape: a growing liberalization. SC L REV 18:254, 1966.

Statutory rape of an insane person, by I. N. Perr. J FORENSIC SCI 13:433-441, October, 1968.

Stop/look/listen/manhunt, by Steel. TAKEOVER 4(2):4, January 31, 1974.

A story of repression and rape. EL GRITO DEL NORTE 4(10): 6, October 28, 1971.

Street walking, by Moon Woman. GOOD TIMES 4(8):4, February 26, 1971.

A study of civil commitment: the Massachusetts sexually dangerous persons act, by A. Louis, et al. HARV J LEG 6:263-306, March, 1969.

Succumbing to rape? by B. Cohn. THE SEC WAVE 2:2.

Summation in case involving assault committed against handicapped female student, by H. B. Glaser. TR LAW Q 6:30, Winter, 1968-1969.

Support grows for Tarboro 3. BLACK PANTH 11(13):7, March 23, 1974.

Supreme court refuses Wansley case. BLACK PANTH 11(23):5, June 1, 1974.

Suspected rape. MED LEG BULL 209:1-4, September, 1970.

Symposium on human sexuality. Sexual trauma of children and

adolescents, by A. W. Burgess, et al. NURS CLIN NORTH AM 10:551-563, September, 1975.

Synopsis of rape for the Florida examiner, by J. R. Feegel. J FL MED ASS 56:729-730, September, 1969.

Terrible trauma of rape, by C. T. Rowan, et al. READ DIGEST 104:198-199+, March, 1974.

They watch motorcycle movies. WOMENS PRESS 1(9):12, October, 1971.

Thomas Wansley political prisoner. SOUTH PAT 29(8):3, October, 1971.

Thoughts on women's conference, by Barnet. PEACEMAK 27(9):4, July 20, 1974.

Three cases of multiple rape, by A. K. Mant. J FORENSIC SCI SOC 4:158-161, March, 1964.

300 years on. ECONOMIST 256:51-52, August 16, 1975.

Tijerina/un crimen brutal. EL GRITO DEL NORTE 4(10):7, October 28, 1971.

To all my sisters. RISING UP ANGRY 3(8):10, December 19, 1971.

To be minor and female, by J. Strouse. MS 1:70-75+, August, 1972.

To kill or be killed. BERKELEY TRIBE 71:18, November 13, 1970.

To stop rape. BERKELEY TRIBE 78:9, January 5, 1971.

Top goal of women's groups: protecting rape victims rights, by B. Keppel. CAL J 5:222-224, July, 1974.

Total health needs of the rape victim, by A. Kaufman, et al. J FAM PRACT 2(3):225-229, June, 1975.

Towards a consent standard in the law of rape. U CHI L REV 43:613-645, Spring, 1976.

Treating terrified rape victims, by L. J. Carbary. J PRACT NURS 24:20-22, February, 1974.

Treating the trauma of rape. HOSP WORLD 2:11-12, April, 1973.

Treatment of sexual offenders in Herstedvester Denmark. The rapists, by G. K. Sturup. ACTA PSYCHIAT SCAND SUPPL 204:5-62, 1968.

Trial near/Hughes feeling pressure. ADVOCATE 46:11, September 11, 1974.

Trial of a rape case: an advocate's analysis of corroboration, consent, and character, by R. A. Hibey. AM CRIM L REV 11:309, Winter, 1973.

TV View/a case of rape, by Brown. GREAT SPECKLED BIRD 7(11):12, March 18, 1974.

Tweeet/Safty in numbers. BERKELEY TRIBE 6(13):6, December 3, 1971.

Twenty times life. BLACK PANTH 5(29):5, January 16, 1971.

Twenty times life, sentence for Charles Collins. TIME 96:46, December 28, 1970.

Twice traumatized: the rape victim and the court, by C. Bohmer, et al. JUDICATURE 58:391-399, March, 1975.

The tyranny of structurelessness, by Joreen. THE SEC WAVE 2:1.

An unusual case of pseudo rape, by A. F. Schiff. J FORENSIC SCI 20(4):637-642, October, 1975.

VA rape frameup continues. GREAT SPECKLED BIRD 7(21): 6, May 27, 1974.

Victim in a forcible rape case—feminist view, by P. L. Wood. AM CRIM L REV 11(2):335-354, 1973.

Victim precipated forcible rape, by M. Amir. J CRIM LAW AND CRIM 58:493-502, December, 1967.

Victimology and rape: the case of the legitimate victim, by K. Weis, et al. ISS CRIM 8(2):71-115, Fall, 1973.

Victimology of rape, by Z. Marek, et al. PRZEGL LEK 31:578-582, 1974.

Victims of rape. BRIT MED J 1(5951):171-172, January 25, 1975.

Victims of rape. BRIT MED J 1(5955):453-454, February 22, 1975.

Victims of rape, by M. C. Korengold. MED ANN DC 40:384, June, 1971.

Victims of sexual assault, by S. Gill. IMPRINT 22(4):24-26, December, 1975.

Violence is a part of the times: interview, by M. A. Lipton. U S NEWS 70:73-74, January 25, 1971.

A visit to the police station, by S. Houstle. COLD DAY IN AUGUST 10.

Waiting on death row, by Lopez. PROGRESS 38(5):38, May, 1974.

Wansley/Carrington appeals denied, by Long. SOUTH PAT 32 (5):3, May, 1974.

Wansley case/a symbol. SOUTH PAT 32(2):5, February, 1974.

The weak are the second sex, by E. Janeway. ATLANTIC MONTH 232:91-104, December, 1973.

What can you say about laws that tell a man: if you rob a

woman you might as well rape her too? by M. W. Lear. REDBK 139:83+, September, 1972.

What every young woman should know about rape, by M. S. Welch. SEVENTEEN 34:146-147+, May, 1975.

What it means to be raped, by K. Whitehorn. OBSERVER 18, June 1, 1975.

What should be the basis for medico-legal diagnosis of defloration, by G. Uribe Cvalla. ZACCHIA 8:1-6, January-March, 1972.

What to do about rape in a third world neighborhood: a white woman's self-criticism, by K. Williams. AIN'T I A WOMAN 3:5, July 20, 1973.

What to do for victims of rape, by C. R. Hayman, et al. RES STAFF PHYSICIAN 19:29-32, August, 1973.

What to do for victims of rape, by C. R. Hayman, et al. MED TIMES 101:47-51, June, 1973.

What women are doing about the ugliest crime, by A. Lake. GOOD H 179:84-85+, August, 1974.

What would you do if, by Morris. PEACE NEWS 19(58):3, February 1, 1974.

When the problem is rape, by B. L. Shaw. RN 35:27-29, April, 1972.

White mans rape. GREAT SPECKLED BIRD 4(12):11, March 22, 1971.

White riot. SEED 7(11):2, November, 1971.

Why we aren't laughing...any more, by N. Weisstein. MS 2:5, November, 1973.

Wives of rapists and incest offenders, by T. B. Garrett, et al. J SEX RES 11(2):149-157, May, 1975.

Women against rape. TIME 101:104, April 23, 1973.

Women hit biased rape laws, by Blakkan. GUARDIAN 26(21): 9, March 6, 1974.

Women hold conference on rape, by Blakkan. GUARDIAN 23(32):6, May 12, 1971.

Women in the struggle. GUARDIAN 24(7):15, November 17, 1971.

Women/know your rights, by Krista. GREAT SPECKLED BIRD 7(16):4, April 22, 1974.

Women move to stop rape, by Hing. ANN ARBOR SUN 2(6): 10, March 22, 1974.

The women of Bangladesh, by J. Goldman. MS 1:84-89, August, 1972.

Women/rape, by Krueger. FREE NEWS 5(3):32, March, 1971.

Women speak out on rape. WOMEN'S WORLD April 15, 1971.

Women together. SEED 6(12):7, May 17, 1971.

Womens auto mechanics ending rape. BROTHER 2:4, March, 1971.

Womens crisis center, by Zwerg. ANN ARBOR SUN 20:4, November 12, 1971.

Womens defense squad. ANN ARBOR SUN 19:3, October 29, 1971.

Women's films/reviving what custom stalled, by M. Haskell. VILLAGE VOICE 17(15):81+, April 13, 1972.

The work of the Criminal Injuries Compensation Board. MEDICOLEG J 34:48-57, 1966.

Worthlessness, disgust, shame: This is the first stage in a woman's reaction to rape, by K. Whitehorn. OBSERVER 17, August 11, 1974.

You asked for it, by D. Borkenhagen. IMPRINT 22:25, December, 1975.

Young girl chaser with motor cycles. Medicolegal study, by A. R. De la Vigne. REV NEUROPSYCHIAT INFANT 20:591-598, June-July, 1972.

PERIODICAL LITERATURE

SUBJECT INDEX

ABORTION

Abortion in case of rape and the code of medical ethics, by L. Ribeiro. HOSPITAL (Rio) 67:9-19, January, 1965.

Certification of rape under the Colorado abortion statute. U COLO L REV 42:121, May, 1970.

Nidation inhibition and abortion following rape, by E. Bohm, et al. MED KLIN 66:989-996, July 2, 1971.

Psychiatric and legal aspects of statutory rape, pregnancy and abortion in juveniles, by M. Shopper. J PSYCH & L 1(3): 275-295, Fall, 1973.

ACQUITTAL

Can a black be acquitted? Indictment of R. Holloway, by N. C. Chriss. NATION 211:690-691, December 28, 1970.

Conviction of secondary party for rape where principal acquitted, by J. R. Scott. LAW QUART 91(364):478-482, 1975.

Criminal law—prosecution for assault with intent to rape is permissable even after a prior acquittal for rape, and a present intent to rape in the future completes the offense. TEX L REV 51:360, January, 1973.

AGGRAVATED RAPE

Aggravated rape, by L. J. Walinsky. NEW REP 173(3):32.

ALCOHOL AND ALCOHOLISM

Alcohol and forcible rape, by M. Amir. BRIT J ADDICT 62:
219-232, December, 1967.

Alcoholism and forcible rape, by R. T. Rada. AM J PSYCH
132:444-446, April, 1975.

Drunkenness as a defence to rape: R. v Vandervoort (OWN
141) and R. v Boucher (2 CCC 241). FAC L REV 22:133,
April, 1964.

ALLEGED RAPE

Alleged rape, an invitational symposium. J REPROD MED 12:
133-144, April, 1974.

False accusations to camouflage autoerotic acts, by F. Kosa.
ARCH KRIMINOL 148:106-110, September-October, 1971.

Medical investigation of alleged rape, by I. Root, et al. WEST J
MED 120:329-333, April, 1974.

The molested young female. Evaluation and therapy of alleged
rape, by J. L. Breen, et al. PEDIATR CLIN NORTH AM
19:717-725, August, 1972.

Review of child molestation and alleged rape cases, by H. A.
Robinson, Jr., et al. AM J OBSTET GYNECOL 110:405-
406, June 1, 1971.

An unusual case of pseudo rape, by A. F. Schiff. J FORENSIC
SCI 20(4):637-642, October, 1975.

ANTI RAPE

Antirape, by Hoffman. ANN ARBOR SUN 2(8):5, April 19, 1974.

Antirape package raped, by Hoffman. ANN ARBOR SUN 2(7): 6, April 5, 1974.

Antirape proposal gains support, by Hoffman. ANN ARBOR SUN 2(6):11, March 22, 1974.

Anti-rape technique: interview, by S. Brownmiller. HARP BAZ 109:119+, March, 1976.

An Atlanta antirape program, by Krista. GREAT SPECKLED BIRD 7(37):6, September 16, 1974.

Atlanta rallies against rape, by Dace. GREAT SPECKLED BIRD 7(34):4, August 26, 1974.

Revolt against rape. TIME 104:85, July 22, 1974.

Revolt against rape; with views of S. Brownmiller. TIME 106: 48+, October 13, 1975.

Women against rape. TIME 101:104, April 23, 1973.

Women move to stop rape, by Hing. ANN ARBOR SUN 2(6): 10, March 22, 1974.

APPEAL

Appeal of Carrington Case, by Lewis. WORK WORLD 16(7): 14, April 5, 1974.

BERG ACID PHOSPHATASE TEST

Modification of the Berg acid phosphatase test, by A. F. Shiff. J FORENSIC SCI 14:538-544, October, 1969.

BIBLIOGRAPHY

Bibliography of hospital emergency departments and trauma units—organization and management, by J. Ryan. BULL AM COLL SURG 60:17-20, September, 1975.

Forcible rape: bibliography, by D. Chappell, et al. J CRIM LAW 65:248-263, June, 1974.

BIOFEEDBACK TREATMENT

Biofeedback treatment of a rape-related psychophysiological cardiovascular disorder, by G. G. Abel, et al. PSYCHOS MED 37(1):85, 1975.

An experimental case study of the bio-feedback treatment of a rape-induced psychophysiological cardiovascular disorder, by E. B. Blanchard, et al. BEH THER 7(1):113-119, January, 1976.

BIRTH CONTROL
see: Pregnancy Prevention

BOOK EXCERPTS

Defending yourself against rape: excerpts from *Our Bodies, Ourselves.* LADIES HOME J 90:62+, July, 1973.

Heroic rapist; excerpt from *Against Our Will: Men, Women and Rape,* by S. Brownmiller. MADEMOISELLE 81:128-129+, September, 1975.

How much do you really know about rapists? excerpt from *Against Rape,* by A. Medea, et al. MS 3:113-114, July, 1974.

How to tell if you're being raped—and what to do about it; excerpt from *The Womansbook,* by V. Billings. REDBK 144: 70+, November, 1974.

BOOK EXCERPTS (cont.)

Rape victim counseling: the legal process; adapted from *Rape: Victims of Crisis,* by A. W. Burgess, et al. J NATL ASSN WOMEN DEANS ADM & COUNSEL 38:24-31, Fall, 1974.

Real spoils of war; excerpt from *Against Our Will: Men, Women and Rape,* by S. Brownmiller. MS 4:82-85, December, 1975.

The role of the victim in sex offenses, by A. Menachem, et al, in SEXUAL BEHAVIORS: SOCIAL CLINICAL AND LEGAL ASPECTS, edited by H. L. Resnik, et al. Boston: Little, Brown, 1972.

BOOK REVIEWS

Against our will—men, women, and rape, by S. Brownmiller, et al. NEW SOC 34(687):556-557, 1975.

—. A review by J. Stafford. ESQUIRE 84:50+, November, 1975.

—. A review by J. Howard. MADEMOISELLE 82:6, January, 1976.

—. A review by H. E. Schwartz. NATION 221:556-558, November, 1975.

Big-house rape—cases, causes and cures, a review of *Rafen in Prison* by A. M. Sacco, by G. M. Farkas. FED PROBAT 39(4):62, 1975.

Crimes of violence—rape and other sex crimes, by F. L. Bailey and H. B. Rothblatt. A review by A. S. Cordon. MISS LAW J 46(3):549-552, 1975.

—. A review by J. R. Galvin. U TOL LAW REV 6(2):570-572, 1975.

Help for rape victim, by B. S. Wallston. CRIM JUST BEH 3(1):103-104, 1976.

BOOK REVIEWS (cont.)

Patterns in forcible rape, by M. Amir. A review by A. J. Reiss, et al. AM J SOC 80(3):785, 1974.

—. A review by R. Lotz. CONT SOC 4(4):381-382, 1975.

Patterns in forcible rape: a review-essay. CRIM L BULL 9:703-710, October, 1973.

Rape in prison, by A. M. Scacco. A review by H. E. Allen. J CRIM JUS 3(4):333-334, 1975.

Rape-offenders and their victims, by J. M. Macdonald. A review by B. Greenspan. FAM COORD 22:257, 1973.

Rape victimology, by L. G. Schultz. A review of H. G. Beigel. J SEX RES 12(1):74, 1975.

—. A review by A. J. Davis. AM J PSYCH 132(12):1341-1342.

—. A review by L. L. Holmstrom. SEX ROLES 1(4):398-400, 1975.

—. A review by A. K. Mant. MED SCI LAW 16(1):76, 1976.

—. A review by F. R. Scarpitti. J MARRIAGE 37(4):1038-1040, 1975.

Rape—victims of crisis, by A. W. Burgess, et al. A review. AM J PSYCH 132(4):462-463.

Reverence to Rape—Treatment of Women in Movies, by M. Haskell, et al. A review. NATION 220(6):182-184, 1975.

Sociology: A Biographical Approach, by P. L. Berger, et al. A review by U. Planck. SOCIOL RUR 15(3):208-209, 1975.

CAPITAL PUNISHMENT

Bikers get death sentence. ADVOC 41:A1, July 3, 1974.

CAPITAL PUNISHMENT (cont.)

Case that could end capital punishment, Maxwell vs Bishop, by R. Hammer. NY TIMES MAG 46-47+, October 12, 1969.

Constitutional law: capital punishment for rape constitutes cruel and unusual punishment when no life is taken or endangered. MINN L REV 56:95, November, 1971.

Constitutional law—death penalty as cruel and unusual punishment for rape. W & M L REV 12:682, Spring, 1971.

Constitutional law—the eighth amendment's proscription of cruel and unusual punishment precludes imposition of the death sentence for rape when the victim's life is neither taken nor endangered. GEO WASH L REV 40:161, October, 1971.

Criminal law rape—death penalty—eighth amendment prohibition against cruel and unusual punishments forbids execution when the victim's life was neither taken nor endangered. U CIN L REV 40:396, Summer, 1971.

Cruel and unusual punishment—constitutionality of the death penalty for rape where victim's life neither taken nor endangered. U RICH L REV 5:392, Spring, 1971.

Death penalty for rape. NATION 200:156-157, February 15, 1965.

Felony, murder, rape and the mandatory death penalty: a study in discretionary justice, by H. A. Bedau. SUFFOLK U L REV 10:493-520, Spring, 1976.

Imposition of the death penalty for rape where the victim's life has been neither taken nor endangered constitutes cruel and unusual punishment under the eighth amendment. HOUS-TON L REV 8:795, March, 1971.

Incidence of the death penalty for rape in Virginia, by D. H. Partington. WASH & LEE L REV 22:43, Spring, 1965.

Lucky death sentence; retrial of Giles brothers. TIME 90:81,

CAPITAL PUNISHMENT (cont.)

November 10, 1967.

My fourteen years on death row, by E. Labat, et al. LOOK 32: 80+, March 19, 1968.

Race, judicial discretion and the death penalty, by M. Wolfgang, et al. ANN AM ACAD POLITIC & SOC SCI 407:119-133, May, 1973.

Rape and death penalty. PEACEMAK 27(6):2, May 4, 1974.

Rape as a capital offense in 19th century Queensland, by R. Barber. AUST J POL 21 (1):31-41, 1975.

Rape, race and the death penalty in Georgia, by M. E. Wolfgang, et al. AM J ORTHOP 45:658-668, July, 1975.

Twenty times life. BLACK PANTH 5(29):5, January 16, 1971.

Twenty times life, sentence for Charles Collins. TIME 96:46, December 28, 1970.

Waiting on death row, by Lopez. PROGRESS 38(5):38, May, 1974.

CASTRATION

Case contribution to the problem of castration of sex offenders hospitalized in a provincial hospital according to paragraph 42b of the German Penal Code, by H. Neumann. NERVEN-ARZT 39:369-375, August, 1968.

On the castration of sexual assailants detained according to paragraph 42b of the German Penal Code, by H. W. Muller, et al. NERVENARZT 39:360-365, August, 1968.

—. Late recurrences, sterilization of criminals detained according to paragraph 42b of the German Penal Code, by A. Langelud-deke. NERVENARZT 39:265-268, August, 1968.

CAUTIONARY INSTRUCTION

Abolishing cautionary instructions in sex offense cases. People vs Rincon-Pineda. CRIM L BULL 12:58-72, January, 1976.

Criminal law—rape—cautionary instruction in sex offense trial relating prosecutrix's credibility to the nature of the crime charged is no longer mandatory; discretionary use in disapproved. FORDHAM URBAN L J 4:419-430, Winter, 1976.

Criminal procedure—instruction to jury that rape is easy to charge and difficult to disprove is no longer to be given. TEX TECH L REV 7:732-737, Spring, 1976.

CHILD RAPE

A case of Heller's dementia following sexual assault in a four-year-old girl, by C. Koupernik, et al. CHILD PSYCH & HUM DEV 2(3):134-144, Spring, 1972.

Child rape: defusing a psychological time bomb, by J. J. Peters. HOSP PHY 9:46-49, February, 1973.

Children who were raped, by A. Katan. PSYCH STUDY OF THE CHILD 28:208-224, 1973.

Female child victims of sex offences, by J. H. Gagnon. SOC PROB 13:176-192, Fall, 1965.

Genital injuries in childhood caused by rape, by J. Schafer, et al. ORV HETIL 113:2245-2246, September 10, 1972.

Indecent assaults on minor girls. Data concerning individuals and environment, by K. G. Stukat. SOCIALMED T 41:437-443, December, 1964.

Lasting psychotic regression in a 4-year-old girl, victim of a rape, by C. Koupernik. REV NEUROPSYCHIAT INFANT SUPPL 63:66, 1967.

The psychic effects of criminal assaults in childhood, by E. Nau.

CHILD RAPE (cont.)

DEUTSCH Z GES GERICHTL MED 55:172-173, September 1, 1964.

Psychosoziale Aspeke von Sexualdelikten an Kindern, by H. Prahm. MSCHR KRIMINOLOGIE & STRAFRECHTSRE-FORM 57:193-198, August, 1974.

Rape: a complex management problem in the pediatric emergency room, by G. L. Lipton, et al. J PEDIAT 75:859-866, November, 1969.

Review of child molestation and alleged rape cases, by H. A. Robinson, Jr., et al. AM J OBSTET GYNECOL 110:405-406, June 1, 1971.

Sex crimes committed against children, by W. Becker. MED KLIN 59:1597-1601, October 2, 1964.

Sexual assault of female children, by V. J. Capraro. ANN NY ACAD SCI 142:817-819, May 10, 1967.

Sexual assault on women and girls, by C. R. Hayman, et al. AM J OBSTET GYNECOL 109:480-486, February 1, 1971.

Sexual assault on women and girls in the District of Columbia, by C. R. Hayman, et al. SOUTH MED J 62:1227-1231, October, 1969.

Sexual assault on women and children in the District of Columbia, by C. R. Hayman, et al. PUB HEALTH REP 83:1021-1028, December, 1968.

Sexual assaults on children, by J. McGeorge. MED SCI LAW 4:245-253, October, 1964.

Sexual assaults on women and girls, by C. R. Hayman. ANN INTERN MED 72:277-278, February, 1970.

Some psychological aspects of seduction, incest, and rape in childhood, by M. Lewis, et al. J AM ACAD CHILD PSYCH

CHILD RAPE (cont.)

8:606-619, October, 1969.

Symposium on human sexuality. Sexual trauma of children and adolescents, by A. W. Burgess, et al. NURS CLIN NORTH AM 10:551-563, September, 1975.

To be minor and female, by J. Strouse. MS 1:70-75+, August, 1972.

CONFERENCES

Alleged rape, an invitational symposium. J REPROD MED 12: 133-144, April, 1974.

Conference on rape. EVERYWOMAN 2(9):2, June 18, 1971.

A conference on rape, by Blakkan. RAD THERAPIST 2(2):6, September, 1971.

Feminists hold rape-defense workshop, by G. Lichtenstein. N Y TIMES 68, April 18, 1971.

New York women discuss rape, by Hardy. MILITANT 35(17): 17, May 7, 1971.

Planning a rape conference, by Kellogg. RAT (20):10, March 2, 1971.

Rape victims tell libbers what it's like, by M. McNellis. N Y SUNDAY NEWS 36, April 18, 1971.

Thoughts on women's conference, by Barnet. PEACEMAK 27(9):4, July 20, 1974.

Women hold conference on rape, by Blakkan. GUARDIAN 23(32):6, May 12, 1971.

CONSENT

Consent and responsibility in sexual offences, by K. L. Koh. CRIM L REV 150-162, March, 1968.

Evidence—admissibility—in a trial for rape, prosecutrix may not be cross examined as to specific acts of prior sexual conduct with men other than defendant, whether the purpose of such cross-examination is to establish her consent as an affirmative defense or to impeach her credibility as a witness. GA L REV 8:973-983, Summer, 1974.

The general opinion still is that anyone who has cheerful sex with a surplus of lovers cannot really be raped, by I. Kurtz. NOVA 9, October, 1975.

If she consented once, she consented again—a legal fallacy in forcible rape cases. VAL U L REV 10:127-167, Fall, 1975.

Indicia of consent? A proposal for change to the common law rule admitting evidence of a rape victim's character for chastity. LOYOLA U L J 7:118-140, Winter, 1976.

Rape and consent. TIME 105:55, May 12, 1975.

Rape, seduction and love—ethics in public and private communication, by C. H. Harpole. SPEECH TEAC 24(4):303-308, 1975.

Some reflections on sexual relations between physicians and patients, by B. Van Emde. J SEX RES 1966.

Towards a consent standard in the law of rape. U CHI L REV 43:613-645, Spring, 1976.

Trial of a rape case: an advocate's analysis of corroboration, consent, and character, by R. A. Hibey. AM CRIM L REV 11:309, Winter, 1973.

CONVICTION

Conviction of secondary party for rape where principal acquitted, by J. R. Scott. LAW QUART 91(364):478-482, 1975.

Fingerprints and criminal conviction, by K. Walker, et al. J COMM PSYCHOL 1(2):192-194, April, 1973.

Other crimes evidence to prove intent in rape cases. LOYOLA L REV 19:751-758, Fall, 1973.

CORROBORATION

Corroborating charges of rape. COLUM L REV 67:1137, June, 1967.

Corroboration in rape cases in New York—a half step forward, by A. B. Goldstein. ALBANY LAW R 37(2):306-328, 1972-1973.

The corroboration rule and crimes accompanying a rape. U PA LAW R 118(3):458-472, 1970.

Nebraska's corroboration rule. NEB L REV 54:93-110, 1975.

Rape corroboration requirement: repeal not reform. YALE L J 81:1365, June, 1972.

Requirements of corroboration in rape cases repealed, by M. Weinstein. QUEEN'S BAR BULL 38:23-28, October, 1974.

Trial of a rape case: an advocate's analysis of corroboration, consent, and character, by R. A. Hibey. AM CRIM L REV 11:309, Winter, 1973.

CRIME RATE

Healthy rise in rape. NEWSWK 80:72, July 31, 1972.

I should have known: it's August, by C. Heimel. MAJ REP

CRIME RATE (cont.)

4:1+, August 22, 1974.

Rape alert, by J. K. Footlick, et al. NEWSWK 86:70-72+, November 10, 1975.

Rape: breaking the silence; with the rising tide of sexual assaults women have organized crisis centers to assist the victims, by M. Wasserman. PROGRESS 37:19-23, November, 1973.

Rape: most rapidly increasing crime, by R. Koenig. MC CALLS 100:25, July, 1973.

Rape wave: creation of rape investigation and analysis section. NEWSWK 81:59, January 29, 1973.

Rise in rape spurs action, by Krista. GREAT SPECKLED BIRD 7(19):5, May 13, 1974.

CRIMINOLOGY

Clinical and research impressions regarding murder and sexually perverse crimes, by L. M. Howell. PSYCHOTHER AND PSYCHOSOM 21(1-6):156-159, 1972-1973.

Criminal violence: inquiries into national patterns and behavior. DISS ABST INTERNATL 33(12-A):7052, June, 1973.

Cultural and sexual differences on the judgement of criminal offences: a replication study of the measurement of delinquency, by M. Hsu. J CRIM LAW & CRIM 64(3):349-353, 1973.

The effect in Philadelphia of Pennsylvania's increased penalties for rape and attempted rape, by B. Schwartz. J CRIM L, CRIMIN POLICE SCIENCE 59(4):509-515, December, 1968.

An exploratory study of five hundred sex offenders, by A. R. Pacht, et al. CRIM JUS BEH 1:13-20, March, 1974.

CRIMINOLOGY (cont.)

Indecent assaults on minor girls. Data concerning individuals and environment, by K. G. Stukat. SOCIALMED T 41:437-443, December, 1964.

Jack A. Gibbens TCN-Rape—22-year cohort study, by K. L. Soothill. MED SCI LAW 16(1):62-69, 1976.

Primitive crimes under the aspects of the evolutional layer therapy and animal behavior research, by K. Jarosch. WIEN KLIN WSCHR 77:757-760, October 15, 1965.

Rape as a heinous but understudied offense, by N. S. Goldner. J CRIM LAW AND CRIM 63:402, September, 1972.

Rape: the victim and the criminal justice system, by L. L. Holmstrom, et al. INTERNATL J CRIM & PENOL 3:101-110, May, 1975.

A statistical evaluation of rape, by A. F. Schiff. J FORENSIC SCI 2:339-349, August, 1973.

Statistical features of rape, by A. F. Schiff. J FORENSIC SCI 14:102-110, January, 1969.

DEFLORATION

Considerations on the subject of defloration, by G. Faraone, et al. ZACCHIA 7:101-118, January-March, 1971.

Defloration. Answer to observations of Professor Uribe Cualla, by G. Faraone, et al. ZACCHIA 8:7-10, January-March, 1972.

What should be the basis for medico-legal diagnosis of defloration, by G. Uribe Cualla. ZACCHIA 8:1-6, January-March, 1972.

DRUG TREATMENT

German drug better than jail. ADVOCATE 72:13, November 10, 1971.

Hormone curbs sex offenders. AM DRUGGIST 159:53, May 5, 1969.

New drug curbs sex urge, by Larsson. GAY 2(63):10, November 8, 1971.

EROTIC STIMULI

Exposure to erotic stimuli and sexual deviance, by M. J. Goldstein. J SOC ISSUES 29(3):197-219, 1973.

False accusations to camouflage autoerotic acts, by F. Kosa. ARCH KRIMINOL 148:106-110, September-October, 1971.

An investigation of the responses of convicted rapists to erotic stimuli, by G. A. Kercher. DISS ABST INTERNATL 32 (1-B):541-542, July, 1971.

Psychodynamics of pornography, by K. S. Walshe-Brennan. NURS MIRROR 142:58-60, January 1, 1976.

Rapists, molesters got less porn. ADVOCATE 50:5, January 6, 1971.

Reactions of convicted rapists to sexually explicit stimuli, by G. A. Kercher, et al. J ABNORM PSYCHOL 8(1):46-50, February, 1973.

Sex books and rape: FBI chief sees close links, by J. E. Hoover, US NEWS 64:14-15, March 11, 1968.

EVIDENCE
    see also: Conviction
                Laws and Legislation
                Medicolegal Problems
                Rape Cases
                Statutory Rape

California rape evidence reform: an analysis of Senate bill 1678.
    HASTINGS L J 26:1551-1573, May, 1975.

Demonstration of spermatozoa in the vaginal smear after criminal
    assault, by W. Spann. DEUTSCH Z GES GERICHTL MED
    55:184-185, September 1, 1964.

Evidence—admissibility—in a trial for rape, prosecutrix may
    not be cross examined as to specific acts of prior sexual con-
    duct with men other than defendent, whether the purpose
    of such cross-examination is to establish her consent as
    an affirmative defense or to impeach her credibility as a
    witness. GA L REV 8:973-983, Summer, 1974.

Evidence—criminal law—prior sexual offenses against a person
    other than the prosecutrix. TUL L REV 46:336, December,
    1971.

Evidence of complainant's sexual conduct in rape cases, by
    G. Zucker. BROOK BARR 27:55-65, November, 1975.

Evidence—presumption that trial judge disregarded incompetent
    evidence in reaching his verdict does not obtain where an
    objection to the evidence has been overruled. LOYOLA U L
    J 2:420, Summer, 1971.

Evidence—rape trials—victim's prior sexual history, by E. G.
    Johnson. BAYLOR L REV 27:362-369, Spring, 1975.

Examination of semen and saliva in a single stain, by L. O. Barse-
    giants. SUD MED EKSPERT 14:30-32, October-December,
    1971.

EVIDENCE (cont.)

Fingerprints and criminal conviction, by K. Walker, et al. J
COMM PSYCHOL 1(2):192-194, April, 1973.

Limitations on the right to introduce evidence pertaining to the
prior sexual history of the complaining witness in cases of
forcible rape: reflection of reality or denial of due process?
HOFSTRA L REV 3:403-426, Spring, 1975.

On the use of a particular technic to make a more precise diagnosis of hymenal integrity, by G. Dellepiana. MINERVA MED-
ICOLEG 84:37-43, May-June, 1964.

Physical evidence in rape cases, by L. R. Vitallo. J POLIC SCI
2(2):160, 1974.

FEMINISM

Arrest feminist at rapists trial, by Kearon. EVERYWOMAN
2(15):7, October 26, 1971.

Arrests feminists at rapist trial, by Kerron. GOODBYE TO ALL
THAT 20:4, October, 1971.

Feminists hold rape-defense workshop, by G. Lichtenstein. N Y
TIMES 68, April 18, 1971.

Our sisters speak. Rape: the response. WOMEN A J OF LIB
3:2.

Rape victims tell libbers what it's like, by M. McNellis. N Y
SUNDAY NEWS 36, April 18, 1971.

Rape: violating the other man's property, by J. Thompson.
BROADSHEET: NEW ZEALAND'S FEM MAG 33:30-33,
October, 1975.

Self defense, preserve of females, by J. Lafferty. J FEM LIB
4:96, April, 1970.

FEMINISM (cont.)

Victim in a forcible rape case—feminist view, by P. L. Wood. AM CRIM L REV 11(2):335-354, 1973.

The weak are the second sex, by E. Janeway. ATLANTIC MONTH 232:91-104, December, 1973.

Why we aren't laughing...any more, by N. Weisstein. MS 2:5, November, 1973.

Women speak out on rape. WOMEN'S WORLD April 15, 1971.

Women's films/reviving what custom stalled, by M. Haskell. VILLAGE VOICE 17(15):81+, April 13, 1972.

FORCIBLE RAPE

Alcohol and forcible rape, by M. Amir. BRIT J ADDICT 62: 219-232, December, 1967.

Alcoholism and forcible rape, by R. T. Rada. AM J PSYCH 132:444-446, April, 1975.

Battery and rape; medico-ethical problems in the examination and reporting to the police, by H. T. Cremers. NED TIJD-SCHR GENEESKD 119(32):1259-1262, August 9, 1975.

Crisis intervention and investigation of forcible rape, by M. Bard, et al. POLICE CHIEF 41(5):68-74, 1974.

Forcible rape, by M. Amir. FED PROBAT 31:51, March, 1967.

Forcible rape and problem of rights of accused, by E. Sagarin. INTELLECT 103(2366):515-520, 1975.

Forcible rape and the criminal justice system: surveying present practices and projecting future trends, by D. Chappell. CRIME & DELINQ 22:125-136, April, 1976.

Forcible rape: bibliography, by D. Chappell, et al. J CRIM LAW

FORCIBLE RAPE (cont.)

AND CRIM 65:248-263, June, 1974.

Forcible rape by multiple offenders, by G. Geis, et al. ABST ON
CRIM & PENOL 11(4):431-436, 1971.

If she consented once, she consented again—a legal fallacy in
forcible rape cases. VAL U L REV 10:127-167, Fall, 1975.

Limitations on the right to introduce evidence pertaining to the
prior sexual history of the complaining witness in cases of
forcible rape: reflection of reality or denial of due process?
HOFSTRA L REV 3:403-426, Spring, 1975.

Recent statutory developments in the definition of forcible rape.
VA L REV 61:1500-1543, November, 1975.

Victim in a forcible rape case—feminist view, by P. L. Wood. AM
CRIM L REV 11(2):335-354, 1973.

Victim precipitated forcible rape, by M. Amir. J CRIM LAW AND
CRIM 58:493-502, December, 1967.

FRAUD

Fraud in assault and rape, by A. Hooper. UBC L REV 3:117,
May, 1968.

GANG RAPE

Clinical study of "plots" (sex crimes committed by gangs), by
P. Parrot, et al. REV NEUROPSYCHIAT INFANT 11:
385-390, July-August, 1963.

Group sexual assaults, by G. Geis. MED ASPECTS OF HUM
SEXUAL 5(5):100-113, May, 1971.

Long Island woman gang raped. GAY 2(58):12, August 30,
1971.

GANG RAPE (cont.)

Social and cultural determinants of the aggressive behavior of the participants in gang rapes, by C. Czapow. PRZEGLAD PENITENJARNY I KRYMINOLOGICZNY 11(1):3-17, 1973.

HEILBRUN

Heilbron draws a veil. ECONOMIST 257:32-33, December 13, 1975.

Heilbron report, by J. C. Smith. CRIM L REV 97:106, February, 1976.

HISTORY

NAWL/IBA program—rapporteur's report, by L. Penland, et al. WOMEN LAW J 60:176-207, Fall, 1974.

The politics of rape—a selective history, by R. Lacks. VILLAGE VOICE February 4, 1971.

Rape and the law in the United States: an historical and sociological analysis, by E. C. Viano. INTERNATL J CRIM & PENOL 2:317-328, November, 1974.

Rape as a capital offense in 19th century Queensland, by R. Barber. AUST J POL 21(1):31-41, 1975.

Sex-crime and its socio-historical background, by F. E. Frenkel. J HIST IDEAS 25:333-352, July, 1964.

Sexual criminality in the early Renaissance: Venice 1338-1358, by G. Ruggiero. J SOC HIST 8:18-37, Summer, 1975.

HITCHIKERS

Beware of female hitchikers, by Wicker. GAY 2(45):4, March 1,

HITCHIKERS (cont.)

1971.

Hitching. ST LOUIS OUTLAW 2(12):20, December 3, 1971.

HOSPITAL EMERGENCY ROOMS

Bibliography of hospital emergency departments and trauma units—organization and management, by J. Ryan. BULL AM COLL SURG 60:17-20, September, 1975.

Crisis intervention in the emergency room for rape victims, by Rev. H. R. Lewis. BULL AM PROTE HOSP ASS 37(2): 112-119, 1973.

Emercency department protocol for management of rape cases, by C. R. Hayman, et al. J AM MED ASS 226:1577-1578, December 24-31, 1973.

Rape: a complex management problem in the pediatric emergency room, by G. L. Lipton, et al. J PEDIAT 75:859-866, November, 1969.

Rape: a plea for help in the hospital emergency room, by C. C. Williams, et al. NURS FORUM 12:338-401, 1973.

Rape—attitudinal training for police and emergency room personnel, by M. L. Keefe, et al. POLICE CHIEF 42(11):36-37, 1975.

Rape victim in the emergency ward, by A. W. Burgess, et al. AM J NURSING 73:1740-1745, October, 1973.

Rape victims—the invisible patients, by V. Price. CAN NURSE 71(4):29-34, April, 1975.

Rape victims: the unpopular patients, by E. LeBourdais. DIMEN HEALTH SERV 53:12-14, March, 1976.

Sexual assault package: a refinement of a previous idea, by P. M.

HOSPITAL EMERGENCY ROOMS (cont.)

Fahrney. J AM COLL EMERGENCY PHYSICIANS 4:340-341, July-August, 1975.

Sexual assault program: District of Columbia, by R. L. Standard. MED ANN DC 41:95-96, February, 1972.

Sexual assault: signs and symptoms, by A. W. Burgess, et al. J EMERGENCY NURSING 1:10-15, March-April, 1975.

Treating terrified rape victims, by L. J. Carbary. J PRACT NURS 24:20-22, February, 1974.

Treating the trauma of rape. HOSP WORLD 2:11-12, April, 1973.

HOSPITALS

Dispute over care of Baltimore County rape victims settled; hospitals to be paid. AM MED NEWS 18:12, August 11, 1975.

Illinois hospitals required to give rape victims free care. HOSP 49:17, September 16, 1975.

Organizing a rape crisis program in a general hospital, by E. Bassuk, et al. J AM MED WOM ASSOC 30(12):486-490, December, 1975.

Rape: hospitals can do more than treat the victim, by H. Freilich. HOSP MED STAFF 4:1-7, September, 1975.

Sexual assault center: Harborview Medical Center, Seattle. HOSP 48:22, June 1, 1974.

HOSPITALS—RAPE IN

Nursing coverage: patient raped by orderly. REGAN REP NURS 16:2, February, 1976.

HOSPITALS—RAPE IN (cont.)

Sexual molestations in hospitals. The role of the physician and other suggestions of managements, by R. Cohen. CLIN PEDIAT 3:689-691, December, 1964.

HYMEN

Do all Filipino women have lacerated hymens?, by P. Anzures. J PHILIPP MED ASS 40:763-764, September, 1964.

Medicolegal examination of the hymen, by A. Debarge, et al. MED LEG DOMM CORPOR 6:298-300, July-September, 1973.

On the use of a particular technic to make a more precise diagnosis of hymenal integrity, by G. Dellepiane. MINERVA MEDICOLEG 84:37-43, May-June, 1964.

Judge and jury attitudes to rape, by R. Barber. AUSTRALIAN & NEW ZEALAND J OF CRIM 7:157-172, September, 1974.

Judicial attitudes toward rape victims, by C. Bohmer. JUDICATURE 57:303-307, February, 1974.

Least punished crime. NEWSWK 80:33, December 18, 1972.

Race, judicial discretion and the death penalty, by M. Wolfgang, et al. ANN AM ACAD POLITIC & SOC SCI 407:119-133, May, 1973.

JUVENILE OFFENDERS

Disposition of juvenile offenders, by B. Green. CRIM L Q 13: 348, June, 1971.

LAWS AND LEGISLATION
see also: Corroboration
Evidence
Medicolegal Problems
Rape Cases
Statutory Rape

Admissibility of a rape-complainant's previous sexual conduct: the need for legislative reform. NEW ENGLAND L REV 11:497-507, Spring, 1976.

The behind-the-scenes story of the unanimous repeal bill victory, by N. Leurs. MAJ REPT 3:6-7, March, 1974.

California, rape evidence reform: an analysis of Senate bill 1678. HASTINGS L J 26:1551-1573, May, 1975.

Certification of rape under the Colorado abortion statute. U COLO L REV 42:121, May, 1970.

Constitutional law: capital punishment for rape constitutes cruel and unusual punishment when no life is taken or endangered. MINN L REV 56:95, November, 1971.

Constitutional law—cruel and unusual punishment. SUFFOLK U L REV 5:504, Winter, 1971.

Constitutional law—death penalty as cruel and unusual punishment for rape. W & M L REV 12:682, Spring, 1971.

Constitutional law—the eighth amendment's proscription of cruel and unusual punishment precludes imposition of the death sentence for rape when the victim's life is neither taken nor endangered. GEO WASH L REV 40:161, October, 1971.

Constitutional law—the Texas equal rights amendments—a rape statute that only punishes men does not violate the Texas ERA. TEX TECH L REV 7:724-731, Spring, 1976.

Constitutionality of the death penalty for non-aggravated rape.

LAWS AND LEGISLATION (cont.)

WASH U L Q 1972:170, Winter, 1972.

Conviction of secondary party for rape where principal acquitted, by J. R. Scott. LAW QUART 91(364):478-482, 1975.

Corroboration in rape cases in New York—a half step forward, by A. B. Goldstein. ALBANY LAW R 37(2):306-328, 1972-1973.

Court changes rape penalty. SOUTH PAT 29(1):7, January, 1971.

The criminal code and rape and sex offenses, by V. A. Lindabury. CAN NURSE 71(4):3, April, 1975.

Criminal law: mistake of age as a defense to statutory rape. U FLA L REV 18:699, Spring, 1966.

Criminal law—prosecution for assault with intent to rape is permissable even after a prior acquittal for rape, and a present intent to rape in the future completes the offense. TEX L REV 51:360, January, 1973.

Criminal law—psychiatric examination of prosecutrix in rape case. NC L REV 45:234, December, 1966.

Criminal law—rape—cautionary instruction in sex offense trial relating prosecutrix's credibility to the nature of the crime charged is no longer mandatory; discretionary use is disapproved. FORDHAM URBAN L J 4:419-430, Winter, 1976.

Criminal law—rape—death penalty—eighth amendment prohibition against cruel and unusual punishments forbids execution when the victim's life was neither taken nor endangered. U CIN L REV 40:396, Summer, 1971.

Criminal procedure—instruction to jury that rape is easy to charge and difficult to disprove is no longer to be given. TEX TECH L REV 7:732-737, Spring, 1976.

Criminal sexual conduct law passes, by Crandell. ANN ARBOR SUN 2(15):4, July 26, 1974.

Cruel and unusual punishment—constitutionality of the death penalty for rape where victim's life neither taken nor endangered. U RICH L REV 5:392, Spring, 1971.

The effect in Philadelphia of Pennsylvania's increased penalties for rape and attempted rape, by B. Schwartz. J CRIM L, CRIMIN POLICE SCIENCE 59(4):509-515, December, 1968.

Evidence—admissibility—in a trial for rape, prosecutrix may not be cross examined as to specific acts of prior sexual conduct with men other than defendant, whether the purpose of such cross-examination is to establish her consent as an affirmative defense or to impeach her credibility as a witness. GA L REV 8:973-983, Summer, 1974.

Evidence—criminal law—prior sexual offenses against a person other than the prosecutrix. TUL L REV 46:336, December, 1971.

Evidence of complainant's sexual conduct in rape cases, by G. Zucker. BROOK BARR 27:55-65, November, 1975.

Evidence—presumption that trial judge disregarded incompetent evidence in reaching his verdict does not obtain where an objection to the evidence has been overruled. LOYOLA U L J 2:420, Summer, 1971.

Felony, murder, rape and the mandatory death penalty; a study in discretionary justice, by H. A. Bedau. SUFFOLK U L REV 10:493-520, Spring, 1976.

Forcible rape and the criminal justice system: surveying present practices and projecting future trends, by D. Chappell. CRIME & DELINQ 22:125-136, April, 1976.

House-of-delegates redefines death, urges redefinition of rape, and undoes Houston amendments. ABA J 61:463-470, April, 1975.

If she consented once, she consented again—a legal fallacy in forcible rape cases. VAL U L REV 10:127-167, Fall, 1975.

Imposition of the death penalty for rape where the victim's life has been neither taken nor endangered constitutes cruel and unusual punishment under the eighth amendment. HOUSTON L REV 8:795, March, 1971.

Indiana's rape shield law: conflict with the confrontation clause? IND L REV 9:418-440, January, 1976.

Indicia of consent? LOYOLA U L J 7:118-140, Winter, 1976.

The law of rape, by F. H. A. Micklewright. LABOUR MO 57: 314-317, July, 1975.

The law on rape, by M. Colton. WOMEN SPEAKING 4(7), July-September, 1975.

Least punished crime. NEWSWK 80:33, December 18, 1972.

Liability to punishment for pregnancy interruptions following rape, in the new penal code?, by H. J. Rieger. DEUTSCH MED WSCHR 94:507, March 7, 1969.

Limitations on the right to introduce evidence pertaining to the prior sexual history of the complaining witness in cases of forcible rape: reflection of realty or denial of due process? HOFSTRA L REV 3:403-426, Spring, 1975.

Males may claim rape under Massachusetts law. ADVOCATE 46:12, September 11, 1974.

Michigan's criminal sexual assault law, by K. A. Cobb, et al. U MICH J L REF 8:217-236, Fall, 1974.

NAWL/IBA program—rapporteur's report, by L. Penland. WO-

LAWS AND LEGISLATION (cont.)

MEN LAW J 60:176-207, Fall, 1974.

Nature and quality of the act: a re-evaluation. OTTAWA L REV 3:340, Fall, 1968.

The new Florida rape law, by A. F. Schiff. J FL MED ASS 62(9):40-42, September, 1975.

Ohio's new rape law: does it protect complainant at the expense of the rights of the accused? AKRON L REV 9:337-359, Fall, 1975.

Proposed amendments to the criminal code with respect to the victims of rape and related sexual offences, by G. R. Goodman. MAN L J 6:275-281, 1975.

Q. If you rape a woman and steal her TV, what can they get you for in New York? A. Stealing her TV, by M.W. Lear. N Y TIMES MAG 10-11+, January 30, 1972; Discussion, 24+, February 27, 1972.

Rape and rape laws: sexism is society and law, by C. E. LeGrand. CALIF L REV 61:919-941, May, 1973.

Rape and the law in the United States: an historical and sociological analysis, by E. C. Viano. INTERNATL J CRIM & PENOL 2:317-328, November, 1974.

Rape corroboration requirement: repeal not reform. YALE L J 81:1365, June, 1972.

Rape law, by Liddell. WOMENS PRESS 1(7):3, August, 1971.

Rape law in Texas: H.B. 284 and the road to reform, by S. Weddington. AM J CRIM L 4:1-14, Winter, 1975-1976.

Rape law revised. GAY LIB 39:3, August, 1974.

Rape law: the need for reform, by R. B. Washburn. NEW MEX L REV 5:279-309, May, 1975.

Rape myths: in legal, theoretical, and everyday practice, by J. R. Schwendinger, et al. CRIME & SOC JUS 1:18-26, Spring-Summer, 1974.

Rape reform legislation: is it the solution? CLEV ST L R 24: 463-503, 1975.

Rape: the victim and the criminal justice system, by L. L. Holmstrom, et al. INTERNATL J CRIM & PENOL 3:101-110, May, 1975.

Rape victim: a victim of society and the law. WILLIAMETTE L J 11:36-55, Winter, 1974.

The rape victim: is she also the unintended victim of the law?, by A. Taylor. N Y TIMES June 15, 1971.

Rape/whom does the law protect, by Mastalli. COLL PRESS SER 45:4, March 20, 1974.

Reasonable mistake as to age—a defense to statutory rape under the new penal code. CONN L REV 2:433, Winter, 1969-1970.

Reasonable mistake of age: a needed defense to statutory rape, by L. W. Myers. MICH L REV 64:105, November, 1965.

A reasoned approach to the reform of sex offense legislation, by R. B. Schram. PROSPECTUS 1:139-161, April, 1968.

Recent statutory developments in the definition of forcible rape. VA L REV 61:1500-1543, November, 1975.

Report to the Hague suggested revisions of penal laws relating to sex crimes and crimes against the family, by M. Ploscowe. CORNELL LAW Q 50:425-445, Spring, 1965.

Requirements of corroboration in rape cases repealed, by M. Weinstein. QUEEN'S BAR BULL 38:23-28, October, 1974.

LAWS AND LEGISLATION (cont.)

Resistance standard in rape legislation. STAN L REV 18:680, February, 1966.

Sex and the law: some officials invoke ancient sex statutes— selectively, critics say, by S. N. Sesser. WALL ST J 172:1, July 5, 1968.

Sexual assault bill, by Rzepka. HERSELF 3(2):13, May, 1974.

Sexual offences act, by Arran. ENCOUNTER 38:3-8, March, 1972.

Sociological, medical and legal aspects of rape, by C. A. Ring- rose. CRIM L Q 17(4):440-445, 1975.

A study in civil commitment: the Massachusetts sexually danger- ous persons act, by A. Louis, et al. HARV J LEG 6:263- 306, March, 1969.

Synopsis of rape for the Florida examiner, by J. R. Feegel. J FL MED ASS 56:729-730, September, 1969.

Towards a consent standard in the law of rape. U CHI L REV 43:613-645, Spring, 1976.

What can you say about laws that tell a man: if you rob a wo- man, you might as well rape her too?, by M. W. Lear. RED- BK 139:83+, September, 1972.

Women hit biased rape laws, by Blakkan. GUARDIAN 26(21): 9, March 6, 1974.

MALE VICTIMS

Males may claim rape under Massachusetts law. ADVOCATE 46:12, September 11, 1974.

MEDICAL ETHICS

Abortion in case of rape and the code of medical ethics, by L. Ribeiro. HOSPITAL (Rio) 67:9-19, January, 1965.

Battery and rape; medico-ethical problems in the examination and reporting to the police, by H. T. Cremers. NED TIJDSCHR GENEESKD 119(32):1259-1262, August 9, 1975.

Sexual crimes and the medical examiner: interview with Milton Helpern. MED ASPECTS HUM SEXUALITY 8(4):161-168, April, 1974.

Some reflections on sexual relations between physicians and patients, by B. Van Emde. J SEX RES 1966.

MEDICOLEGAL PROBLEMS
    see also: Evidence
             Laws and Legislation
             Rape Cases
             Statutory Rape

Battery and rape; medico-ethical problems in the examination and reporting to the police, by H. T. Cremers. NED TIJDSCHR GENEESKD 119(32):1259-1262, August 9, 1975.

Evaluation and differentiation of the penal responsibility of the sex offender, by H. Hinderer. PSYCHIATR NEUROL MED PSYCHOL 25:257-265, May, 1973.

Medico-legal considerations on the presence of a tampax in the vaginal orifice during a rape, by P. L'Epee, et al. MED LEG DOMM CORPOR 1:180-181, April, 1968.

Medicolegal examination of the hymen, by A. Debarge, et al. MED LEG DOMM CORPOR 6:298-300, July-September, 1973.

The professional as a court witness, by A. W. Burgess, et al.

MEDICOLEGAL PROBLEMS (cont.)

J EMERGENCY NURS 2:25-30, March-April, 1976.

Rape needs a special examination, by A. F. Schiff. EMER MED 3:28-29, October, 1971.

Standard rape investigation form, by W. F. Enos, et al. VA MED MON 101:43-44, January, 1974.

Suspected rape. MED LEG BULL 209:1-4, September, 1970.

What should be the basis for medico-legal diagnosis of defloration, by G. Uribe Cualla. ZACCHIA 8:1-6, January-March, 1972.

The work of the Criminal Injuries Compensation Board. MEDICOLEG J 34:48-57, 1966.

Young girl chasers with motorcycles. Medicolegal study, by A. R. De la Vigne. REV NEUROPSYCHIATR INFANT 20: 591-598, June-July, 1972.

MORNING AFTER PILL
    see: Pregnancy-Prevention

MOTORCYCLISTS

Bikers get death sentence. ADVOCATE 41:A1, July 3, 1974.

They watch motorcycle movies. WOMENS PRESS 1(9):12, October, 1971.

Young girl chasers with motorcycles. Medicolegal study, by A. R. De la Vigne. REV NEUROPSYCHIATR INFANT 20: 591-598, June-July, 1972.

MOVIES

Heads or tails: Women in American Movies and Society, a review of *From Reverence to Rape: the Treatment of Women in the Movies,* by M. Haskell. A review by D. J. Gorssvogel. DIACRIT 5(3):49-55, Fall, 1975.

Rape—an ugly movie trend, by A. Harmetz. N Y TIMES, ARTS & LEIS September 30, 1973.

They watch motorcycle movies. WOMENS PRESS 1(9):12, October, 1971.

Women's films/reviving what custom stalled, by M. Haskell. VILLAGE VOICE 17(15):81+, April 13, 1972.

MULTIPLE RAPE

Three cases of multiple rape, by A. K. Mant. J FORENSIC SCI SOC 4:158-161, March, 1964.

MURDER

Clinical and research impressions regarding murder and sexually perverse crimes, by L. M. Howell. PSYCHOTHER & PSY-CHOSOM 21(1-6):156-159, 1972-1973.

Felony, murder, rape and the mandatory death penalty: a study in discretionary justice, by H. A. Bedau. SUFFOLK U L REV 10:493-520, Spring, 1976.

Motive for murder. ECONOMIST 225:71, April 12, 1975.

Murder. ST LOUIS OUTLAW 1(13):2, March 5, 1971.

Night of rape and death in jail. ADVOCATE 40:12, June 19, 1974.

The series rapist Bernhard N. Report on a murderer released

MURDER (cont.)

from prison, by G. Bauer. ARCH KRIMINOL 147:65-73, March-April, 1971.

To kill or be killed. BERKELEY TRIBE 71:18, November 13, 1970.

NON-AGGRAVATED RAPE

Constitutionality of the death penalty for non-aggravated rape. WASH U L Q 1972:170, Winter, 1972.

PERSONAL ETHICS
    see: Consent
           Victims—Character and Credibility

PERSONAL NARRATIVES

I'll tell you what its like in jail, by Johnston. GAY 2(64):4, November 22, 1971.

Like Ann's gynecologist or time I was almost raped—personal narratives in womens rap groups, by S. Kalcik. J AM FOLK-LO 88(347):3-11, 1975.

My fourteen years on death row, by E. Labat, et al. LOOK 32:80+, March 19, 1968.

My husband was accused of rape: case of mistaken identity. GOOD H 178:16+, April, 1974.

PHYSICAL INJURY

Forcible laceration of the rectum, by P. Altunkov, et al. KHIR-URGIIA 23:167-169, 1970.

Genital injuries in childhood caused by rape, by J. Schafer, et al.

PHYSICAL INJURY (cont.)

ORV HETIL 113:2245-2246, September 10, 1972.

Injuries during coitus, by M. Chomakov, et al. AKUSH GINEK 4:223-227, 1965.

POLICE
    see also: Evidence
             Laws and Legislation
             Medicolegal Problems
             Rape Cases
             Statutory Rape

Crisis intervention and investigation of forcible rape, by M. Bard, et al. POLICE CHIEF 41(5):68-74, 1974.

Law enforcement's participation in crisis counseling for rape victims, by J. Stratton. POLICE CHIEF 43(3):46-49, 1976.

Police discretion and the judgment that a crime has been committed—rape in Philadelphia. U PA LAW R 117:277, December, 1968.

Police processing of rape complaints: a case study. AM J CRIM L 4:15-30, Winter, 1975-1976.

Rape and police protection, by Hutchinson. GREAT SPECKLED BIRD 4(42):5, October 18, 1971.

Rape—attitudinal training for police and emergency room personnel, by M. L. Keefe, et al. POLICE CHIEF 42(11):36-37, 1975.

Rape squad: Manhattan sex crimes squad, by G. Lichtenstein. N Y TIMES MAG 10-11+, March 3, 1974; Reply by S. Baumgarten, 73, April 14, 1974.

Rape wave: creation of rape investigation and analysis section. NEWSWK 81:59, January 29, 1973.

POLICE (cont.)

St. Louis trains policewomen/rape squad. FOCUS—MIDWEST
9(60):6, nd.

A visit to the police station, by S. Houstle. COLD DAY IN
AUGUST 10.

PORNOGRAPHY
see: EROTIC STIMULI

PREGNANCY

Liability to punishment for pregnancy interruptions following
rape, in the new penal code?, by H. J. Rieger. DEUTSCH
MED WSCHR 94:507, March 7, 1969.

A note on stress and sex determination, by I. Wittles, et al. J
GEN PSYCHOL 124(2):333-334, June, 1974.

Psychiatric and legal aspects of statutory rape, pregnancy and
abortion in juveniles, by M. Shopper. J PSYCH & L 1(3):
275-295, Fall, 1973.

PREGNANCY—PREVENTION

Abortion in case of rape and the code of medical ethics, by L.
Ribeiro. HOSPITAL (Rio) 67:9-19, January, 1965.

Afterthoughts on the morning—after pill, by K. Weiss. MS 2:5,
November, 1973.

DES: Banned for cattle and prescribed for women, by E. Frankfort. VILLAGE VOICE 7, March 22, 1973.

Estrogen therapy after rape?, by B. Paulshock, et al. ANN IN-
TERN MED 72:961, June, 1970.

Nidation inhibition and abortion following rape, by E. Bohm,

PREGNANCY-PREVENTION (cont.)

et al. MED KLIN 66:989-996, July 2, 1971.

Postcoital estrogens in cases of rape, by M. G. Chapman. NEW ENG J MED 280:277, January 30, 1969.

PRESS COVERAGE

Black man, white woman—the maintenance of a myth: rape and the press in New Orleans, by D. J. Abbott, et al., in CRIME AND DELINQUENCY, by M. Riedel. Praeger, 1974, pp. 141-153.

High count backs naming of rape victims in news. ED & PUB 108:11+, March 8, 1975.

Rape victim's picture and name front paged, by C. M. Rupp. ED & PUB 108:8, May 31, 1975.

Right to privacy; overturning of a Georgia stature forbidding publication of a rape victim's name, by J. K. Footlick, et al. NEWSWK 85:66, March 17, 1975.

Singles rapist makes the daily news. MAJ REP 4(7):3, July 25, 1974.

PRISON

I'll tell you what its like in jail, by Johnston. GAY 2(64):4, November 22, 1971.

Jail is like another world, by B. Calvert. WIN 6(14):11, September 1, 1970.

PRISON—RAPE IN

Deadly sex games in prison, by Dennis. ADVOCATE 44:25, August 14, 1974.

PRISON—RAPE IN (cont.)

In defense of Sis Joanne: for ourselves and history, by M. R. Karenga. BLACK SCHOLAR 6:37-42, July, 1975.

Joanne Little: America goes on trial. FREEDOMWAYS 15(2): 87-88, August, 1975.

Joanne Little: the dialectics of rape, by A. Davis. MS 3:74-77+, June, 1975.

Night of rape and death in jail. ADVOCATE 40:12, June 19, 1974.

PROSECUTION

Bringing the rapist to trial, a group effort, by C. Price. WOMEN'S WORLD 1:3, November-December, 1971.

Criminal law—prosecution for assault with intent to rape is permissable even after a prior acquittal for rape, and a present intent to rape in the future completes the offense. TEX L REV 51:360, January, 1973.

Justice for Franca; challenging Mafia traditions by prosecuting her abductor in Sicily. NEWSWK 69:37, January 2, 1967.

NAWL/IBA program—rapporteur's report, by L. Penland. WOMEN LAW J 60:176-207, Fall, 1974.

The professional as a court witness, by A. W. Burgess, et al. J EMERGENCY NURS 2:25-30, March-April, 1976.

Twice traumatized: the rape victim and the court, by C. Bohmer, et al. JUDICATURE 58:391-399, March, 1975.

PSYCHOPHYSIOLOGICAL CARDIOVASCULAR DISORDER

Biofeedback treatment of a rape-related psychophysiological

PSYCHOPHYSIOLOGICAL CARDIOVASCULAR
DISORDER (cont.)

cardiovascular disorder, by G. G. Abel, et al. PSYCHOS
MED 37(1):85, 1975.

An experimental case study of the bio-feedback treatment of a
rape-induced psychophysiological cardiovascular disorder, by
E. B. Blanchard, et al. BEH THER 7(1):113-119, January,
1976.

RACISM

Being an Asian in Texas, worth 20 years. PEOPLES WORLD
34(21):8, May 22, 1971.

Black charged with raping white, by Grant. SOUTH PAT 29(8):
6, October, 1971.

Black man, white woman—the maintenance of a myth: rape and
the press in New Orleans, by D. J. Abbott, et al., in CRIME
AND DELINQUENCY, by M. Riedel. Praeger, 1974, pp.
141-153.

Can a black be acquitted? Indictment of R. Holloway, by N.
C. Chriss. NATION 211:690-691, December 28, 1970.

Chicana rape victim fights indictment. BLACK PANTH 12(4):
9, August 17, 1974.

In defense of Sis Joanne: for ourselves and history, by M. R.
Karenga. BLACK SCHOLAR 6:37-42, July, 1975.

Joanne Little: America goes on trial. FREEDOMWAYS 15(2):
87-88, 1975.

Joanne Little: the dialectics of rape, by A. Davis. MS 3:74-77+,
June, 1975.

Mississippi justice; white man's life imprisonment. NEWSWK
66:42, November 22, 1965.

RACISM (cont.)

On black women, by A. Davis. MS 1:55+, August, 1972.

Race, judicial discretion and the death penalty, by M. Wolfgang, et al. ANN AM ACAD POLITIC & SOC SCI 407:119-133, May, 1973.

Racist use of rape charge, by Golos. WORK WORLD 16(10):11, May 17, 1974.

Racist use of rape charge, by Hardin. SOUTH PAT 32(7):3, September, 1974.

Racist use of rape laws, by Smith. MILITANT 38(24):12, June 21, 1974.

Rape and social structure, by D. Lester. PSYCHOL REP 35(1): 146, 1974.

Rape and the Harlem woman: she asked for it—or did she?, by M. Walker. MAJ REP 4:1+, August 22, 1974.

Rape, race and the death penalty in Georgia, by M. E. Wolfgang, et al. AM J ORTHOP 45:658-668, July, 1975.

The sex offenses of blacks and whites, by S. A. Kirk. ARCH OF SEX BEH 4(3):295-302, May, 1975.

What to do about rape in a third world neighborhood: a white woman's self-criticism, by K. Williams. AIN'T I A WOMAN 3:5, July 20, 1973.

RAPE

Aftermath of rape, by W. H. Masters, et al. REDBK 147:74+, June, 1976.

Aspects of rape, by K. Lindsey, et al. THE SEC WAVE 2:2.

Attack on women, by J. H. Court. AUSTRALAS NURSES J

RAPE (cont.)

4:1+, September, 1975.

Code R, for rape. NEWSWK 80:75, November 13, 1972.

Couple-speak: rape, true and false, by S. de Gramont, et al. VOGUE 157:108+, June, 1971.

Crime of rape, by H. B. Shaffer. ED RES REPTS 43-60, January 19, 1972.

The crime of rape in the Albuquerque area, by B. Turpen. DIV GOVT RES R (U N MEX) 83:1-4, January, 1975.

Expertise in sex crimes, by R. Djordjic, et al. SRPSKI ARH CELOK LEK 97:159-166, February, 1969.

Is rape a sex crime?, by D. Ben-Horin. NATION 221:112-115, August 16, 1975.

The offense of rape in Victoria, by E. J. Hodgens, et al. AUS-TRALIAN & NEW ZEALAND J OF CRIM 5(4):225-240, 1972.

On rape, by D. Densmore. NO MORE FUN AND GAMES 6: 57-84, May, 1973.

One reading of rape, by C. Macinnes. NEW SOC 33(667):147, July 17, 1975.

Rape. EVERYWOMAN 1(14):8, February 5, 1971.

Rape. MEDICOLEG J 44(1):1-5, 1976.

Rape, by G. Sheridan, et al. GUARDIAN 11, January 15, 1975.

Rape, by J. Selkin. PSYCHOL TODAY 8:70-72+, January, 1975.

Rape. GAY LIBERATOR 39:1, August, 1974.

RAPE (cont.)

Rape. NORTHWEST PASS 11(4):24, July 29, 1974.

Rape. OTHER WOMAN 2(5):12, June, 1974.

Rape. OTHER WOMAN 2(6):2, July, 1974.

Rape, by R. Hartman. ILL MED J 145:518-519, June, 1974.

Rape. HARRY 2(18):9, August 16, 1971.

Rape. FIFTH ESTATE 5(24):17, April 1, 1971.

Rape. NOLA EXPRESS 1(55):3, May 15, 1970.

Rape: a normal act?, by R. G. Kasinsky. CAN FORUM 55: 18-22, September, 1975.

Rape: a 22-year cohort study, by K. L. Soothill, et al. MED SCI LAW 16(1):62-69, January, 1976.

Rape alert, by J. K. Footlick, et al. NEWSWK 86:70-72+, November 10, 1975.

Rape, an analysis, by Nett. WOMENS PRESS 1(6):10, July, 1971.

Rape and other sexual offenses, by J. Barnes. BRIT MED J 2:293-295, April 29, 1967.

Rape and social structure, by D. Lester. PSYCHOL REP 35(1): 146, 1974.

Rape and what to do about it, by J. Kole. HARP BAZ 109: 118-119+, March, 1976.

Rape as a heinous but understudied offense, by N. S. Goldner. J CRIM LAW AND CRIM 63:402, September, 1972.

Rape/crime of violence, by Krista. GREAT SPECKLED BIRD 7(10):3, March 11, 1974.

RAPE (cont.)

Rape: exploding the myths, by E. Bernstein, et al. TODAYS HEALTH 53:36-39+, October, 1975.

Rape is a four-letter word, by M. R. Schulz. ETC 32:65-69, March, 1975.

Rape: most rapidly increasing crime, by R. Koenig. MC CALLS 100:25, July, 1973.

Rape: no woman is immune, by C. See. TODAYS HEALTH 53:30, October 5, 1975.

Rape reality, rape fantasy; discussion, by P. Steinfels. COMMONWEAL 102:554+, November 21, 1975.

—. COMMONWEAL 103:59-61+, January 16, 1976.

Rape: the all-American crime, by S. Griffin. RAMP 10:26-35, September, 1971.

Rape: the medical, social, and legal implications, by J. R. Evrard. AM J OBSTET GYNECOL 111:197-199, September 15, 1971.

Rape: the unmentionable crime, by A. Lake. GOOD H 173: 104-105+, November, 1971.

Rape: when to fight back, by J. Selkin. PSYCHOL TODAY 8:70-72+, January, 1975.

Sex-'n-'violence, by B. Brophy. NEW STATESM 69:677-678, April 30, 1965.

Sex offenses and sex offenders, by D. E. J. MacNamara. ANN AM ACAD POLITIC & SOC SCI 376:148-155, March, 1968.

The sex offenses of blacks and whites, by S. A. Kirk. ARCH OF SEX BEH 4(3):295-302, May, 1975.

Sexual assault on women and girls, by C. R. Hayman, et al.

RAPE (cont.)

AM J OBSTET GYNECOL 109:480-486, February 1, 1971.

Sexual assaults on women and girls, by C. R. Hayman. ANN INTERN MED 72:277-278, February, 1970.

Simple question of rape, by S. Alexander. NEWSWK 84:110, October 28, 1974.

Sociological, medical and legal aspects of rape, by C. A. Ringrose. CRIM L Q 17(4):440-445, 1975.

Violence is a part of the times: interview, by M. A. Lipton. U S NEWS 70:73-74, January 25, 1971.

What every young woman should know about rape, by M. S. Welch. SEVENTEEN 34:146-147+, May, 1975.

When the problem is rape, by B. L. Slaw. RN 35:27-29, April, 1972.

RAPE—AUSTRALIA

Attack on women, by J. H. Court. AUSTRALAS NURSES J 4:1+, September, 1975.

Rape as a capital offense in 19th century Queensland, by R. Barber. AUST J POL 21(1):31-41, 1975.

RAPE—BANGLADESH

Raped women of Bangladesh, by B. Karkaria. ILL WEEKLY OF INDIA 93:14-17, June 18, 1972.

The women of Bangladesh, by J. Goldman. MS 1:84-89, August, 1972.

RAPE—CANADA

The case against Steven Truscott in Canada, by K. Simpson. MEDICOLEG J 36:Suppl 4:58-71, 1968.

RAPE—DENMARK

Treatment of sexual offenders in Herstedvester Denmark. The rapists, by G. K. Sturup. ACTA PSYCHIAT SCAND SUPPL 204:5-62, 1968.

RAPE—FOREIGN COUNTRIES

Rape in foreign countries, by A. F. Schiff. MED TRIAL TECHN QUART 20:66-74, 1974.

—. MED TRIAL TECHN QUART 20:66-64, Summer, 1973.

Rape in other countries, by A. F. Schiff. MED SCI LAW 1(3): 139-143, 1971.

RAPE—GERMANY

Case contribution to the problem of castration of sex offenders hospitalized in a provincial hospital according to paragraph 42b of the German Penal Code, by H. Neumann. NERVEN-ARZT 39:369-375, August, 1968.

On the castration of sexual assailants detained according to paragraph 42b of the German Penal Code, by H. W. Muller, et al. NERVENARZT 39:360-365, August, 1968.

On the castration of sexual assailants: late recurrences; sterilization of criminals detained according to paragraph 42b of the German Penal Code, by A. Langeluddeke. NERVENARZT 39:265-268, August, 1968.

RAPE—GREAT BRITAIN

The law of rape (Great Britain), by F. H. A. Micklewright. LABOUR MO 57:314-317, July, 1975.

RAPE—ITALY

Sexual criminality in the early Renaissance: Venice 1338-1358, by G. Ruggiero. J SOC HIST 8:18-37, Summer, 1975.

RAPE—NEW ZEALAND

The offense of rape in Victoria, by E. J. Hodgens, et al. AUSTRALIAN & NEW ZEALAND J OF CRIM 5(4):225-240, 1972.

Rape: violating the other man's property, by J. Thompson. BROADSHEET: NEW ZEALAND'S FEM MAG 33:30-33, October, 1975.

RAPE—PHILIPPINES

Do all Filipino women have lacerated hymens?, by P. Anzures. J PHILIPP MED ASS 40:763-764, September, 1964.

RAPE—SINGAPORE

The pattern of rape in Singapore, by A. Y. Ng. SINGAPORE MED J 15:49-50, March, 1974.

RAPE—UNITED STATES

Sex offenses and sex offenders, by D. E. J. MacNamara. ANN AM ACAD POLITIC & SOC SCI 376:148-155, March, 1968.

RAPE—UNITED STATES—CALIFORNIA

California rape evidence reform: an analysis of Senate bill 1678. HASTINGS L J 26:1551-1573, May, 1975.

Top goal of women's groups: protecting rape victims rights, by B. Keppel. CAL J 5:222-224, July, 1974.

RAPE—UNITED STATES—COLORADO

Certification of rape under the Colorado abortion statute. U COLO L REV 42:121, May, 1970.

RAPE—UNITED STATES—DISTRICT OF COLUMBIA

The mental health committee: report of the Subcommittee on the problem of rape in the District of Columbia, by E. H. Weiss, et al. MED ANN DC 41:703-704, November, 1972.

Rape in the District of Columbia, by C. R. Hayman, et al. AM J OBSTET GYNECOL 113:91-97, May 1, 1972.

Sexual assault on women and children in the District of Columbia, by C. R. Hayman, et al. PUB HEALTH REP 83:1021-1028, December, 1968.

Sexual assault on women and girls in the District of Columbia, by C. R. Hayman, et al. SOUTH MED J 62:1227-1231, October, 1969.

Sexual assault program: District of Columbia, by R. L. Standard. MED ANN DC 41:95-96, February, 1972.

RAPE—UNITED STATES—FLORIDA

The new Florida rape law, by A. F. Schiff. J FL MED ASS 62(9):40-42, September, 1975.

Synopsis of rape for the Florida examiner, by J. R. Feegel. J FL

RAPE–UNITED STATES–FLORIDA (cont.)

MED ASS 56:729-730, September, 1969.

RAPE–UNITED STATES–GEORGIA

An Atlanta antirape program, by Krista. GREAT SPECKLED BIRD 7(37):6, September 16, 1974.

Atlanta rallies against rape, by Dace. GREAT SPECKLED BIRD 7(34):4, August 26, 1974.

Grady rape crisis center, by Krista. GREAT SPECKLED BIRD 7(26):13, July 1, 1974.

Rape, race and the death penalty in Georgia, by M. E. Wolfgang, et al. AM J ORTHOP 45:658-668, July, 1975.

Right to privacy; overturning of a Georgia statute forbidding publication of a rape victim's name, by J. K. Footlick, et al. NEWSWK 85:66, March 17, 1975.

RAPE–UNITED STATES–ILLINOIS

Illinois hospitals required to give rape victims free care. HOSP 49:17, September 16, 1975.

Rape in Illinois: a denial of equal protection. JOHN MARSHAL J 8:457-496, Spring, 1975.

RAPE–UNITED STATES–INDIANA

Indiana's rape shield law: conflict with the confrontation clause? IND L REV 9:418-440, January, 1976.

RAPE–UNITED STATES–MARYLAND

Dispute over care of Baltimore County rape victims settled;

RAPE—UNITED STATES—MARYLAND (cont.)

hospitals to be paid. AM MED NEWS 18:12, August 11, 1975.

Rape case that shook Maryland: Giles case, by T. W. Lippman. REPORT 38:32-34, March 7, 1968.

Rashomon in Maryland: Giles-Johnson rape case, by S. Brownmiller. ESQUIRE 69:130-132+, May, 1968.

RAPE—UNITED STATES—MASSACHUSETTS

Males may claim rape under Massachusetts law. ADVOCATE 46:12, September 11, 1974.

A study in civil commitment: the Massachusetts sexually dangerous persons act, by A. Louis, et al. HARV J LEG 6:263-306, March, 1969.

RAPE—UNITED STATES—MICHIGAN

Michigan's criminal sexual assault law, by K. A. Cobb, et al. U MICH J L REF 8:217-236, Fall, 1974.

RAPE—UNITED STATES—MISSISSIPPI

Mississippi justice; white man's life imprisonment. NEWSWK 66:42, November 22, 1965.

RAPE—UNITED STATES—MISSOURI

Missouri justices red faced. ADVOCATE 70:19, October 13, 1971.

RAPE—UNITED STATES—NEBRASKA

Nebraska's corroboration rule. NEB L REV 54:93-110, 1975.

RAPE—UNITED STATES—NEW MEXICO

The crime of rape in the Albuquerque area, by B. Turpen. DIV GOVT RES R (U N MEX) 83:1-4, January, 1975.

RAPE—UNITED STATES—NEW YORK

Corroboration in rape cases in New York—a half step forward, by A. B. Goldstein. ALBANY LAW R 37(2):306-328, 1972-1973.

Q. If you rape a woman and steal her TV, what can they get you for in New York? A. Stealing her TV, by M. W. Lear. N Y TIMES MAG 10-11+, January 30, 1972; discussion 24+, February 27, 1972.

Rape squad: Manhattan sex crimes squad, by G. Lichtenstein. N Y TIMES MAG 10-11+, March 3, 1974; reply by S. Baumgarten, 73, April 14, 1974.

RAPE—UNITED STATES—OHIO

Ohio's new rape law: does it protect complainant at the expense of the rights of the accused? AKRON L REV 9:337-359, Fall, 1975.

RAPE—UNITED STATES—PENNSYLVANIA

The effect in Philadelphia of Pennsylvania's increased penalties for rape and attempted rape, by B. Schwartz. J CRIM L, CRIM IN POLICE SCIENCE 59(4):509-515, December, 1968.

Police discretion and the judgment that a crime has been com-

RAPE—UNITED STATES—PENNSYLVANIA (cont.)

mitted—rape in Philadelphia. U PA LAW R 117:277, December, 1968.

RAPE—UNITED STATES—TEXAS

Constitutional law—the Texas equal rights amendment—a rape statute that only punishes men does not violate the Texas ERA. TEX TECH L REV 7:724-731, Spring, 1976.

Rape law in Texas: H.B. 284 and the road to reform, by S. Weddington. AM J CRIM L 4:1-14, Winter, 1975-1976.

RAPE—UNITED STATES—VIRGINIA

Incidence of the death penalty for rape in Virginia, by D. H. Partington. WASH & LEE L REV 22:43, Spring, 1965.

RAPE—UNITED STATES—WASHINGTON

Sexual assault center: Harborview Medical Center, Seattle. HOSP 48:22, June 1, 1974.

RAPE CASES
   see also: Laws and Legislation
             Medicolegal Problems

Abolishing cautionary instructions in sex offense cases: People v. Rincon-Pineda. CRIM L BULL 12:58-72, January, 1976.

Appeal of Carrington Case, by Lewis. WORK WORLD 16(7): 14, April 5, 1974.

Can a black be acquitted? Indictment of R. Holloway, by N. C. Chriss NATION 211:690-691, December 28, 1970.

The case against Steven Truscott in Canada, by K. Simpson.

RAPE CASES (cont.)

MEDICOLEG J 36:Suppl 4:58-71, 1968.

Case that could end capital punishment: Maxwell vs Bishop, by R. Hammer. N Y TIMES MAG 46-47+, October 12, 1969.

Centenary reflections on Prince's case, by R. Cross. L Q REV 91:540-553, October, 1975.

D.P.P. vs Morgan 2 WLR 913. L Q REV 91:478-482, October, 1975.

Drunkenness as a defense to rape: R. vs Vandervoort (O W N 141) and R. vs Boucher (2 C C C 241). FAC L REV 22: 133, April, 1974.

Free Wansley now. SOUTH PAT 32(1):1, January, 1974.

Giles vs Maryland. 87 Sup Ct 793. J URBAN L 46:118, 1968.

Girl's reputation: J. Roberts vs Giles brothers. TIME 86:44, August 6, 1965.

Hughes held for trial. ADVOCATE 35:12, April 10, 1974.

In defense of Sis Joanne: for ourselves and history, by M. R. Karenga. BLACK SCHOLAR 6:37-42, July, 1975.

Inez Garcia on trial, by N. Blitman, et al. MS 3:49-54+, May 1975.

Joanne Little: America goes to trial. FREEDOMWAYS 15(2): 87-88, 1975.

Joanne Little: the dialectics of rape, by A. Davis. MS 3:74-77+, June, 1975.

Judge rescinds order to close rape hearing. ED & PUB 108:33, July 5, 1975.

Justice for Franca; challenging Mafia traditions by prosecuting

RAPE CASES (cont.)

her abductor in Sicily. NEWSWK 69:37, January 2, 1967.

Lucky death sentence; retrial of Giles brothers. TIME 90:81, November 10, 1967.

People vs English 209 N E 2d 722. BROOK L REV 32:434, April, 1966.

People vs Hernandez. 393 P 2d 673.

—in ALA L REV 17:101, Fall, 1964.
AM CRIM L Q 4:57, Fall, 1965.
ARIZ L REV 7:324, Spring, 1966.
CATHOLIC U L REV 14:123, January, 1965.
DE PAUL L REV 14:449, Spring-Summer, 1965.
DENVER L J 41:322, September-October, 1964.
GA SB J 1:552, May 1965.
GEO L J 53:506, Winter, 1965.
GEO WASH L REV 33:588, December, 1964.
HARV L REV 78:1257, April, 1965.
HASTINGS L J 16:270, November, 1964.
IA L REV 50:628, Winter, 1965.
J FAMILY L 5:107, Spring, 1965.
MINN L REV 50:170, November, 1965.
MISS L J 36:254, March, 1965.
MONTANA L REV 26:133, Fall, 1964.
NC L REV 43:424, February, 1965.
ND L REV 41:59, November, 1964.
ORE L REV 44:243, April, 1965.
SO CALIF L REV 38:131, 1965.
STAN L REV 17:309, January, 1965.
SYRACUSE L REV 16:148, Fall, 1964.
U COLO L REV 37:295, Winter, 1965.
UMKC L REV 33:158, Winter, 1965.
VAND L REV 18:244, December, 1964.
W VA L REV 67:149, February, 1965.
WASH & LEE L REV 22:119, Spring, 1965.
WASHBURN L J 5:141, Winter, 1965.
WAYNE L REV 11:556, Winter, 1965.

RAPE CASES (cont.)

People vs Lombardi. 229 N E 2d 206. ST JOHN'S L REV 42:604, April, 1968.

People vs Rincon-Pineda, rape trials depart the seventeenth century—farewell to Lord Hale. TULSA L J 11:279-290, 1975.

Pride of Inez Garcia, by M. Del Drago. MS 3:54+, May, 1975.

Rape case that shook Maryland: Giles case, by T. W. Lippman. REPORT 38:32-34, March 7, 1968.

The rape of Sheila Robinson, by R. Bruce. IMPRINT 22:32-33+, December, 1975.

Rashomon in Maryland. Giles-Johnson rape case, by S. Brown-miller. ESQUIRE 69:130-132+, May, 1968.

Regina vs Schell. No. 88 of 1964, Law Society Reports, Tas. TAS U L REV 2:202, November, 1965.

Return of the phantom; arrest of M. Brookins. NEWSWK 74:24, July 14, 1969.

Self-defense against rape: the Joanne Little case, by J. Bond. BLACK SCHOLAR 6:29-31, March, 1975.

The series rapist Bernhard N. Report on a murderer released from prison, by G. Bauer. ARCH KRIMINOL 147:65-73, March-April, 1971.

A slight case of rape, by A. Watkins. SPECTATOR 225, August 20, 1965.

Summation in case involving assault committed against handicapped female student, by H. B. Glaser. TR LAW Q 6:30, Winter, 1968-1969.

Support grows for Tarboro 3. BLACK PANTH 11(13):7, March 23, 1974.

RAPE CASES (cont.)

Supreme court refuses Wansley case. BLACK PANTH 11(23):5, June 1, 1974.

Thomas Wansley political prisoner. SOUTH PAT 29(8):3, October, 1971.

Trial near/Hughes feeling pressure. ADVOCATE 46:11, September 11, 1974.

Twenty times life; sentence for Charles Collins. TIME 96:46, December 28, 1970.

Wansley/Carrington appeals denied, by Long. SOUTH PAT 32(5):3, May, 1974.

Wansley case/a symbol. SOUTH PAT 32(2):5, February, 1974.

RAPE CRISIS CENTERS

Dealing with rape, by H. Newman. THE SEC WAVE 2:3.

Development of a medical-center rape crisis-intervention program, by S. L. McCombie. AM J PSYCH 133(4):418-421, 1976.

Establishment of a rape crisis center, by G. E. Robinson, et al. CAN MENT HEALTH 23(5):10-12, September, 1975.

For the rapist's victim, a place of sanctuary and sympathy, by B. Yoklavich. DAILY TELEGRAPH 17, May 23, 1975.

Grady rape crisis center, by Krista. GREAT SPECKLED BIRD 7(26):13, July 1, 1974.

Organizing a rape crisis program in a general hospital, by E. Bassuk, et al. J AM MED WOM ASSOC 30(12):486-490, December, 1975.

Rape: breaking the silence; with the rising tide of sexual assaults

RAPE CRISIS CENTERS (cont.)

women have organized crisis centers to assist the victims, by
M. Wasserman. PROGRESS 37:19-23, November, 1973.

Rape treatment centers set up in two cities. J AM MED ASS
233:11+, July 7, 1975.

Sexual asault center: Harborview Medical Center, Seattle.
HOSP 48:22, June 1, 1974.

Womens crisis center, by Zwerg. ANN ARBOR SUN 20:4,
November 12, 1971.

RAPE IN LITERATURE

Caryatid: war, rape and masculine consciousness, by A. Rich.
AM POETRY REV 2:10-11, May-June, 1973.

The oral rape fantasy and rejection of mother in the imagery of
Shakespeare's Venus and Adonis, by A. B. Rothenberg.
PSYCHOANAL Q 40:447-468, 1971.

Rape in literature, by C. A. Douglas. THE SEC WAVE 2:2.

RAPE PREVENTION

Avoiding rape: whose advise should you take?, by N. Gittelson.
MC CALLS 103:66, May, 1976.

How can a woman avoid rapd?, by E. Mason. INTELLECT
103:512-513, May, 1975.

How to keep from being raped, by C. West. PROGRESS WO-
MEN 2:16, April 2, 1972.

How to protect yourself from rape. GOOD H 181:157, September, 1975.

Rape prevention tactics. MS 3:114-115, July, 1974.

RAPE PREVENTION (cont.)

Rape squad: Manhattan sex crimes sqad, by G. Lichtenstein. N Y TIMES MAG 10-11+, March 3, 1974; reply by S. Baumgarten, 73, April 14, 1974.

Safety in the home, by Price, et al. MAJ REP 4(7):2, July 25, 1974.

St. Louis trains policewomen/rape squad. FOCUS-MIDWEST 9(60):6, nd.

To stop rape. BERKELEY TRIBE 78:9, January 5, 1971.

What every young woman should know about rape, by M. S. Welch. SEVENTEEN 34:146-147+, May, 1975.

Womens defense squad. ANN ARBOR SUN 19:3, October 29, 1971.

RAPE TRAUMA SYNDROME
see: Trauma

RAPISTS

Age of the culprits and the injured in sex offenses, by I. Klose. DEUTSCH Z GES GERICHTL MED 59:129-134, 1967.

Daylight prowlers, by J. Steele. GUARDIAN 11, November 26, 1975.

Disposition of juvenile offenders, by B. Green. CRIM L Q 13: 348, June, 1971.

An exploratory study of five hundred sex offenders, by A. R. Pacht, et al. CRIM JUS BEH 1:13-20, March, 1974.

How much do you really know about rapists? excerpt from *Against Rape,* by A. Medea, et al. MS 3:113-114, July, 1974.

RAPISTS (cont.)

An investigation of the responses of convicted rapists to erotic stimuli, by G. A. Kercher. DISS ABST INTERNATL 32 (1-B):541-542, July, 1971.

My husband was accused of rape: case of mistaken identity. GOOD H 178:16+, April, 1974.

On the castration of sexual assailants: late recurrences; sterilization of criminals detained according to paragraph 42b of the German Penal Code, by A. Langeluddeke. NERVENARZT 39:265-268, August, 1968.

Personality characteristics of rapists, by W. C. Perdue, et al. PERCEP & MOTOR SKILLS 35(2):514, October, 1972.

Portrait of a rapist. NEWSWK 82:67, August 20, 1973.

The public image of the sex offender, by G. J. Falk. MENT HYG 48:612-620, October, 1964.

Rapists, molesters got less porn. ADVOCATE 50:5, January 6, 1971.

Sex offenses and sex offenders, by D. E. J. MacNamara. ANN AM ACAD POLITIC & SOC SCI 376:148-155, March, 1968.

Sexualstraftater, by E. Schorsch. ENKE 230-249, 1971.

Wives of rapists and incest offenders, by T. B. Garrett, et al. J SEX RES 11(2):149-157, May, 1975.

RAPISTS—CRIMINAL RECORD

Evidence—criminal law—prior sexual offenses against a person other than the prosecutrix. TUL L REV 46:336, December, 1971.

Forcible rape by multiple offenders, by G. Geis, et al. ABST ON CRIM & PENOL 11(4):431-436, 1971.

RAPISTS—CRIMINAL RECORD (cont.)

Other crimes evidence to prove intent in rape cases. LOYOLA L
REV 19:751-758, Fall, 1973.

RAPISTS—LEGAL RIGHTS

Evidence—criminal law—prior sexual offenses against a person
other than the prosecutrix. TUL L REV 46:336, December,
1971.

Forcible rape and problem of rights of accused, by E. Sagarin.
INTELLECT 103(2366):515-520, 1975.

Ohio's new rape law: does it protect complainant at the expense of the rights of the accused? AKRON L REV 9:337-
359, Fall, 1975.

Rape in Illinois: a denial of equal protection. JOHN MARSHAL
J 8:457-496, Spring, 1975.

Rape/whom does the law protect, by Mastalli. COLL PRESS
SER 45:4, March 20, 1974.

RAPISTS—PSYCHOLOGY

Adequacy of ego functioning in rapists and pedophiles, by T. K.
Seghorn. DISS ABST INTERNATL 31(12-B):7613-7614,
June, 1971.

Evaluation and differentiation of the penal responsibility of the
sex offender, by H. Hinderer. PSYCHIATR NEUROL MED
PSYCHOL 25:257-265, May, 1973.

Heroic rapist: excerpt from *Against Our Will: Men, Women and
Rape,* by S. Brownmiller. MADEMOISELLE 81:128-129+,
September, 1975.

The modification of sexual fantasies: a combined treatment
approach to the reduction of deviant sexual behavior, by W.

RAPISTS—PSYCHOLOGY (cont.)

L. Marshall. BEH RES & THER 11(4):557-564, November, 1973.

Nocturnal penile tumescence and sleep of convicted rapists and other prisoners, by I. Karacan, et al. ARCH OF SEX BEH 3(1):19-26, January, 1974.

The oral rape fantasy and rejection of mother in the imagery of Shakespear's Venus and Adonis, by A. B. Rothenberg. PSYCHOANAL Q 40:447-468, 1971.

Personality characteristics of rapists, by W. C. Perdue, et al. PERCEP & MOTOR SKILLS 35(2):514, 1972.

Psychological needs of rapists, by G. Fisher, t al. BRIT J CRIM 11:182-185, April, 1971.

The psychology of rapists, by M. L. Cohen, et al. SEMIN PSYCH 3(3):307-327, August, 1971.

Rape: a compulsion to destroy, by W. Brombert, et al. MED INSIGHT 6:20-22, April, 1974.

Reactions of convicted rapists to sexually explicit stimuli, by G. A. Kercher, et al. J ABNORM PSYCHOL 81(1):46-50, February, 1973.

RAPISTS—TREATMENT

Hormone curbs sex offenders. AM DRUGGIST 159:53, May 5, 1969.

The modification of sexual fantasies: a combined treatment approach to the reduction of deviant sexual behavior, by W. L. Marshall. BEH RES & THER 11(4):557-564, November, 1973.

New drug curbs sex urge, by Larsson. GAY 2(63):10, November 8, 1971.

RAPISTS—TREATMENT (cont.)

Treatment of sexual offenders in Herstedvester Denmark. The rapists, by G. K. Sturup. ACTA PSYCHIAT SCAND SUPPL 204:5-62, 1968.

REPORTING RAPE

Battery and rape: medico-ethical problems in the examination and reporting to the police, by H. T. Cremers. NED TIJD-SCHR GENEESKD 119(32):1259-1262, August 9, 1975.

How rape is reported, by K. Soothill, et al. NEW SOC 702-704, June 19, 1975.

Jack A.—How rape is reported, by K. Soothill. NEW SOC 32 (663):702-704, 1975.

Sexual crimes and the medical examiner: interview with Milton Helpern. MED ASPECTS HUM SEXUAL 8(4):161-168, April, 1974.

SELF DEFENSE

Defending yourself against rape: excerpts from *Our Bodies, Ourselves.* LADIES HOME J 90:62+, July, 1973.

Don't take it lying down, by C. W. Offir. PSYCHOL TODAY 8:73, January, 1975.

In defense of Sis Joanne: for ourselves and history, by M. R. Karenga. BLACK SCHOLAR 6:37-42, July, 1975.

Joanne Little: America goes on trial. FREEDOMWAYS 15(2): 87-88, 1975.

Joanne Little: the dialectics of rape, by A. Davis. MS 3:74-77+, June, 1975.

Nonviolent self defense, by Morris. WIN 10(2):8, January 24,

SELF DEFENSE (cont.)

1974.

Rape and self defense. SEED 7(11):31, November, 1971.

Rape and self defense. GREAT SPECKLED BIRD 7(11):12, March 18, 1974.

Rape: when to fight back, by J. Selkin. PSYCHOL TODAY 8:70-72+, January, 1975.

Resistance standard in rape legislation. STAN L REV 18:680, February, 1966.

Self-confidence/self-defense, by S. Cordell. THE SEC WAVE 2:4.

Self defense. GAY LIBERATOR 34:6, February, 1974.

Self-defense against rape: the Joanne Little case, by J. Bond. BLACK SCHOLAR 6:29-31, March, 1975.

Self defense class. WOMENS PRESS 4(1):17, February, 1974.

Self defense, preserve of females, by J. Lafferty. J FEM LIB 4:96, April, 1970.

Succumbing to rape?, by B. Cohn. THE SEC WAVE 2:2.

To kill or be killed. BERKELEY TRIBE 71:18, November 13, 1970.

Womens defense squad. ANN ARBOR SUN 19:3, October 19, 1971.

SEX FANTASY

The modification of sexual fantasies: a combined treatment approach to the reduction of deviant sexual behavior, by W. L. Marshall. BEH RES & THER 11(4):557-564, November,

SEX FANTASY (cont.)

1973.

The oral rape fantasy and rejection of mother in the imagery of Shakespeare's Venus and Adonis, by A. B. Rothenberg. PSYCHOANAL Q 40:447-468, 1971.

Psychology constructs the female; or the fantasy life of the male psychologist (with some attention to the fantasies of his friends, the male biologist and the male anthropologist), by N. Weisstein. SOC ED 35(4):362-373, April, 1971.

Rape fantasies, by S. H. Kardener. J REL & HEALTH 14(1): 50-57, January, 1975.

Rape reality, rape fantasy; discussion, by P. Steinfels. COMMONWEAL 102:554+, November 21, 1975.

—. COMMONWEAL 103:59-61+, January 16, 1976.

SEXISM
    see: Social Attitudes

SOCIAL ATTITUDES

Apathy/word of a gentleman, by Williams. MAJ REPT 4(9):3, August 22, 1974.

Attribution of fault to a rape victim as a function of respectability of the victim, by C. Jones, et al. J PER AND SOC PSYCHOLOGY 26(3):415-419, June, 1973.

Black man, white woman—the maintenance of a myth: rape and the press in New Orleans, by D. J. Abbott, et al., in CRIME AND DELINQUENCY, by M. Riedel. Praeger, 1974, pp. 141-153.

But what do we do with our rage?, by G. Steinem. MS 3:51, May, 1975.

SOCIAL ATTITUDES (cont.)

Coming out of dark ages, by Hing. ANN ARBOR SUN 2(2):10, January 25, 1974.

Consciousness-raising on rape and violence, by J. Walker. WOMBAT 1:1, February, 1972.

Do rape victims get what they deserve? NEW HUMAN 89:314, January, 1974.

Female university student and staff perceptions of rape, by M. H. Herman, et al. J NATL ASSN WOMEN DEANS ADM & COUNSEL 38:20-23, Fall, 1974.

Four questions about sex in our society, by J. Kirk. MED TIMES 102(11):68-80, November, 1974.

The general opinion still is that anyone who has cheerful sex with a surplus of lovers cannot really be raped, by I. Kurtz. NOVA 9, October, 1975.

Heroic rapist: excerpt from *Against Our Will: Men, Women and Rape,* by S. Brownmiller. MADEMOISELLE 81:128-129+, September, 1975.

Is rape a sex crime?, by D. Ben-Horin. NATION 221:112-115, August 16, 1975.

Is rape what women really want?, by C. Calvert. MADEMOISELLE 78:134-135+, March, 1974.

It is always the woman who is raped, by D. Metzger. AM J PSYCH 133:405-408, April, 1976.

Judge and jury attitudes to rape, by R. Barber. AUSTRALIAN & NEW ZEALAND J OF CRIM 7:157-172, September, 1974.

NAWL/IBA program—rapporteur's report, by L. Penland, et al. WOMEN LAW J 60:176-207, Fall, 1974.

SOCIAL ATTITUDES (cont.)

Natural law and unnatural acts, by J. M. Finnis. HEYTHROP J 11:365-387, October, 1970.

Nature and quality of the act: a re-evaluation. OTTAWA L REV 3:340, Fall, 1968.

Nice girls don't get into trouble, by G. Sheehy. N Y MAG February 15, 1971.

Nice girls don't get raped, do they?, by E. Paris. CHATELAINE 44:31, 70-72+, September, 1971.

Normal, healthy and pleasureable, by R. Moody. PEACE NEWS 17(95):6, November 20, 1970.

Psychology constructs the female; or the fantasy life of the male psychologist (with some attention to the fantasies of his friends, the male biologist and the male anthropologist) by N. Weisstein. SOC ED 35(4):362-373, April, 1971.

The public image of the sex offender, by G. J. Falk. MENT HYG 48:612-620, October, 1964.

Putting the sex back into rape, by T. Branch. WASH M 8:56-62, March, 1976.

Rape: a normal act?, by R. G. Kasinsky. CAN FORUM 55:18-22, September, 1975.

Rape and rape laws: sexism in society and law, by C. E. Le Grand. CALIF L REV 61:919-941, May, 1973.

Rape and social structure, by D. Lester. PSYCHOL REP 35(1): 146, 1974.

Rape and the fallen woman, by Griffin. EVERYWOMAN 2(15): 1, October 26, 1971.

Rape and the Harlem woman: she asked for it—or did she?, by M. Walker. MAJ REPT 4:1+, August 22, 1974.

SOCIAL ATTITUDES (cont.)

Rape and the law in the United States: an historical and sociological analysis, by E. C. Viano. INTERNATL J CRIM & PENOL 2:317-338, November, 1974.

Rape—attitudinal training for police and emergency room personnel, by M. L. Keefe, et al. POLICE CHIEF 42(11):36-37, 1975.

Rape: exploding the myths, by E. Bernstein, et al. TODAYS HEALTH 53:36-39+, October, 1975.

Rape is a four-letter word, by M. R. Schulz. ETC 32:65-69, March, 1975.

Rape is an ugly word. EMER MED 3:23-27, October, 1971.

Rape myths: in legal, theoretical, and everyday practice, by J. R. Schwendinger, et al. CRIME & SOC JUS 1:18-26, Spring-Summer, 1974.

Rape: no woman is immune, by C. See. TODAYS HEALTH 53:30, October 5, 1975.

Rape: the all-American crime, by S. Griffin. RAMP 10:26-35, September, 1971.

Rape: the double standard, by L. Kuby. APHRA 5:31-35, Winter, 1973-1974.

Rape: the man-made myth, by S. Griffin. NOVA 68-71, December, 1971.

Rape: the medical, social, and legal implications, by J. R. Evrard. AM J OBSTET GYNECOL 111:197-199, September 15, 1971.

Rape: the ultimate violation of the self, by E. Hilberman. AM J PSYCH 133:436-437, April, 1976.

Rape: the unmentionable crime, by A. Lake. GOOD H 173:

SOCIAL ATTITUDES (cont.)

104-105+, November, 1971.

Rape: the victim as defendant, by S. Landau. TRIAL 10:19+, July-August, 1974.

Rape victim: a victim of society and the law. WILLAMETTE L J 11:36-55, Winter, 1974.

Rape victims—the invisible patients, by V. Price. CAN NURSE 71(4):29-34, April, 1975.

Rape victims: the unpopular patients, by E. LeBourdais. DI-MEN HEALTH SERV 53:12-14, March, 1976.

Rape: violating the other man's property, by J. Thompson. BROADSHEET: NEW ZEALAND'S FEMINIST MAG 33: 30-33, October, 1975.

Sex-crime and its socio-historical background, by F. E. Frenkel. J HIST IDEAS 25:333-352, July, 1964.

Sexual liberation and the adolescent girl, by F. Lieberman. BIRTH FAM J 2:51-56, Spring, 1975.

Social, legal, and psychological effects of rape on the victim, by J. J. Peters. PA MED 78(2):34-36, February, 1975.

Society blamed for sexual assaults, by M. Goldstein. NEWS-DAY 15A, April 19, 1971.

Sociological, medical and legal aspects of rape, by C. A. Ring-rose. CRIM L Q 17(4):440-445, 1975.

The weak are the second sex, by E. Janeway. ATLANTIC MONTH 232:91-104, December, 1973.

What can you say about laws that tell a man: if you rob a woman, you might as well rape her too?, by M. W. Lear. REDBK 139:83+, September, 1972.

SOCIAL ATTITUDES (cont.)

What it means to be raped, by K. Whitehorn. OBSERVER 18, June 1, 1975.

What to do about rape in a third world neighborhood: a white woman's self-criticism, by K. Williams. AIN'T I A WOMAN 3:5, July 20, 1973.

Women's films/reviving what custom stalled, by M. Haskell. VILLAGE VOICE 17(15):81+, April 13, 1972.

You asked for it, by D. Borkenhagen. IMPRINT 22:25, December, 1975.

SPERM IDENTIFICATION

Application of a dye used in histology for the purpose of identification of spermatozoids in sperm stains on fabrics, by G. Squillaci. ACTA MED LEG SOC 17:69-70, April-June, 1964.

Immunological method of establishing the presence and species of seminal stains, by V. P. Chernov. SUD MED EKSPERT 14:28-30, October-December, 1971.

Sperm identification—acid phosphatase test, by A. F. Schiff. MED TRIAL TECHN QUART 21(4):467-474, Spring, 1975.

STATUTORY RAPE
  see also: Laws and Legislation
          Medicolegal Problems
          Rape Cases

Criminal law: mistake of age as a defense to statutory rape. U FLA L REV 18:699, Spring, 1966.

Psychiatric and legal aspects of statutory rape, pregnancy and abortion in juveniles, by M. Shopper. J PSYCH & L 1(3): 275-295, Fall, 1973.

STATUTORY RAPE (cont.)

Reasonable mistake as to age—a defense to statutory rape under the new penal code. CONN L REV 2:433, Winter, 1969-1970.

Reasonable mistake of age: a needed defense to statutory rape, by L. W. Myers. MICH L REV 64:105, November, 1965.

Reasonable rape: statutory rape. TIME 87:49, January 21, 1966.

Statutory rape: a critique. LA L REV 26:105, December, 1965.

Statutory rape: a growing liberalization. SC L REV 18:254, 1966.

Statutory rape of an insane person, by I. N. Perr. J FORENSIC SCI 13:433-441, October, 1968.

SYPHILLIS

Serological tests for syphillis in rape cases. J AM MED ASS 228:1227-1228, June 3, 1974.

Serological tests for syphillis in rape cases, by M. I. Greenberg. J AM MED ASS 227:1381, March 25, 1974.

TEMPORAL EPILEPSY

Critical disorders of sex behavior in temporal epilepsy, by G. D'Agata, et al. RASS NEUROPSICHIATR 22:191-204, April-June, 1968.

TRAUMA

Aftermath of rape, by W. H. Masters, et al. REDBK 147:74+, June, 1976.

TRAUMA (cont.)

Assessing trauma in the rape victim, by L. L. Holmstrom, et al. AM J NURSING 75:1288-1291, August, 1975.

Bibliography of hospital emergency departments and trauma units—organization and management, by J. Ryan. BULL AM COLL SURG 60:17-20, September, 1975.

The first half-hour, by L. Appell, et al. J PRACT NURS 26:16-18+, January, 1976.

Rape and the trauma of inadequate care, by M. S. Welch. PRISM 3:17+, September, 1975.

Rape trauma syndrome, by A. W. Burgess, et al. AM J PSYCH 131(9):981-986, September, 1974.

—. NURS DIGEST 3:17-19, May-June, 1975.

Rape victim in the emergency ward, by A. W. Burgess, et al. AM J NURSING 73:1740-1745, October, 1973.

Sexual assault: signs and symptoms, by A. W. Burgess, et al. J EMERGENCY NURSING 1:10-15, March-April, 1975.

Symposium on human sexuality. Sexual trauma of children and adolescents, by A. W. Burgess, et al. NURS CLIN NORTH AM 10:551-563, September, 1975.

Terrible trauma of rape, by C. T. Rowan, et al. READ DIGEST 104:198-199+, March, 1974.

Treating terrified rape victims, by L. J. Carbary. J PRACT NURS 24:20-22, February, 1974.

Treating the trauma of rape. HOSP WORLD 2:11-12, April, 1973.

Twice traumatized: the rape victim and the court, by C. Bohmer, et al. JUDICATURE 58:391-399, March, 1975.

VICTIMOLOGY

Victimology and rape: the case of the legitimate victim, by K. Weis, et al. ISS IN CRIM 8(2):71-115, Fall, 1973.

Victimology of rape, by Z. Marek, et al. PRZEGL LEK 31: 578-582, 1974.

VICTIMS
see also: Male Victims

Age of the culprits and the injured in sex offenses, by I. Klose. DEUTSCH Z GES GERICHTL MED 59:129-134, 1967.

Characteristics of rape victims seen in crisis-intervention, by S. L. McCombie. SMITH COLL 46(2):137-158, 1976.

Coping behavior of the rape victim, by A. W. Burgess, et al. AM J PSYCH 133:413-418, April, 1976.

For victims of rape: many new types of help. US NEWS 79:44, December 8, 1975.

How to help raped, by J. Gilley. NEW SOC 28(612):756-758, 1974.

How you can help the rape victim. NURSING '74 4:11, October, 1974.

Interagency service network to meet needs of rape victims, by G. Hardgrove. SOC CASE 57(4):245-253, 1976.

Judicial attitudes toward rape victims, by C. Bohmer. JUDICA-TURE 57:303-307, February, 1974.

Management of sexually assaulted females, by J. B. Massey, et al. OBSTET GYNECOL 38:29-36, July, 1971.

Rape—the ultimate invasion of privacy, by L. C. Cottell. FBI L ENFORCE BULL 43(5):2-6, 1974.

VICTIMS (cont.)

Rape victim guidelines. MOD HEALTH CARE 3(3):74, March, 1975.

Rape victims: reasons, responses, and reforms, by P. A. Hartwig, et al. INTELLECT 103:507-511, May, 1975.

Raped women of Bangladesh, by B. Karkaria. ILL WEEKLY OF INDIA 93:14-17, June 18, 1972.

The role of the victim in sex offenses, by A. Menachem, et al, in SEXUAL BEHAVIORS: SOCIAL CLINICAL AND LEGAL ASPECTS, edited by H. L. Resnik, et al. Boston: Little Brown, 1972.

Seven who were raped, by B. Donadio, et al. NURS OUTLOOK 22:245-247, April, 1974.

Social, legal, and psychological effects of rape on the victim, by J. J. Peters. PA MED 78(2):34-36, February, 1975.

Victim in a forcible rape case—feminist view, by P. L. Wood. AM CRIM L REV 11(2):335-354, 1973.

Victimology and rape: the case of the legitimate victim, by K. Weis, et al. ISS CRIM 8(2):71-115, Fall, 1973.

Victims of rape. BRIT MED J 1(5951):171-172, January 25, 1975.

Victims of rape. BRIT MED J 1(5955):453-454, February 22, 1975.

Victims of rape, by M. C. Korengold. MED ANN DC 40:384, June, 1971.

Victims of sexual assault, by S. Gill. IMPRINT 22(4):24-26, December, 1975.

What it means to be raped, by K. Whitehorn. OBSERVER 18, June 1, 1975.

VICTIMS (cont.)

Worthlessness, disgust, shame: this is the first stage in a woman's reaction to rape, by K. Whitehorn. OBSERVER 17, August 11, 1974.

VICTIMS—CHARACTER AND CREDIBILITY

Admissibility of a rape-complainant's previous sexual conduct: the need for legislative reform. NEW ENGLAND L REV 11: 497-507, Spring, 1976.

Attribution of fault to a rape victim as a function of respectability of the victim, by C. Jones, et al. J PER AND SOC PSYCHOLOGY 26(3):415-419, June, 1973.

Criminal law—rape—cautionary instruction in sex offense trial relating prosecutrix's credibility to the nature of the crime charged is no longer mandatory; discretionary use is disapproved. FORDHAM URBAN L J 4:419-430, Winter, 1976.

Do rape victims get what they deserve? NEW HUMAN 89:314, January, 1974.

Evidence—admissibility—in a trial for rape, prosecutrix may not be cross examined as to specific acts of prior sexual conduct with men other than defendant, whether the purpose of such cross-examination is to establish her consent as an affirmative defense or to impeach her credibility as a witness. GA L REV 8:973-983, Summer, 1974.

Evidence of complainant's sexual conduct in rape cases, by G. Zucker. BROOK BARR 27:55-65, November, 1975.

Evidence—rape trials—victim's prior sexual history, by E. G. Johnson. BAYLOR L REV 27:362-369, Spring, 1975.

The general opinion still is that anyone who has cheerful sex with a surplus of lovers cannot really be raped, by I. Kurtz. NOVA 9, October, 1975.

Girl's reputation: J. Roberts vs Giles brothers. TIME 86:44, August 6, 1965.

Indicia of consent? A proposal for change to the common law rule admitting evidence of a rape victim's character for chastity. LOYOLA U L J 7:118-140, Winter, 1976.

Limitations on the right to introduce evidence pertaining to the prior sexual history of the complaining witness in cases of forcible rape: reflection of reality or denial of due process? HOFSTRA L REV 3:403-426, Spring, 1975.

Nice girls don't get into trouble, by G. Sheehy. N Y MAG February 15, 1971.

Nice girls don't get raped, do they?, by E. Paris. CHATELAINE 44:31, 70-72+, September, 1971.

Rape and the fallen woman, by Griffin. EVERYWOMAN 2(15): 1, October 26, 1971.

Rape and the Harlem woman: she asked for it—or did she?, by M. Walker. MAJ REP 4:1+, August 22, 1974.

Rape victim: a victim of society and the law. WILLAMETTE L J 11:36-55, Winter, 1974.

Trial of a rape case: an advocate's analysis of corroboration, consent, and character, by R. A. Hibey. AM CRIM L REV 11: 309, Winter, 1973.

Victim precipated forcible rape, by M. Amir. J CRIM LAW AND CRIM 58:493-502, December, 1967.

You asked for it, by D. Borkenhagen. IMPRINT 22:25, December, 1975.

VICTIMS—CHILDREN
see also: Child Rape

A case of Heller's dementia following sexual assault in a four-year-old girl, by C. Koupernik, et al. CHILD PSYCH AND HUM DEV 2(3):134-144, Spring, 1972.

Child rape: defusing a psychological time bomb, by J. J. Peters. HOSP PHY 9:46-49, February, 1973.

Children who were raped, by A. Katan. PSYCH STUDY OF THE CHILD 28:208-224, 1973.

Female child victims of sex offenses, by J. H. Gagnon. SOC PROB 13:176-192, Fall, 1965.

Genital injuries in childhood caused by rape, by J. Schafer, et al. ORV HETIL 113:2245-2246, September 10, 1972.

Lasting psychotic regression in a 4-year-old girl, victim of a rape, by C. Koupernik. REV NEUROPSYCHIAT INFANT SUPPL 64:66, 1967.

The psychic effects of Criminal assaults in childhood, by E. Nau. DEUTSCH Z GES GERICHTL MED 55:172-173, September 1, 1964.

Psychosoziale Aspeke von Sexualdelikten an Kindern, by H. Prahm. MSCHR KRIMIN & STRAFRECHTSREFORM 57:193-198, August, 1974.

Some psychological aspects of seduction, incest, and rape in childhood, by M. Lewis, et al. J AM ACAD CHILD PSYCH 8:606-619, October, 1969.

Symposium on human sexuality. Sexual trauma of children and adolescents, by A. W. Burgess, et al. NURS CLIN NORTH AM 10:551-563, September, 1975.

VICTIMS—COUNSELING

Aftermath of rape, by W. H. Masters, et al. REDBK 147:74+,

June, 1976.

Characteristics of rape victims seen in crisis-intervention, by S. L. McCombie. SMITH COLL 46(2):137-158, 1976.

Counseling rape victims, by Rev. R. S. Crum. J PASTORAL CARE 28:112-121, June, 1974.

Crisis and counseling requests of rape victims, by A. W. Burgess, et al. NURSING RES 23:196-202, May-June, 1974.

Crisis intervention and investigation of forcible rape, by M. Bard, et al. POLICE CHIEF 41(5):68-74, 1974.

Crisis intervention in the emergency room for rape victims, by Rev. H. R. Lewis. BULL AM PROTE HOSP ASS 37(2): 112-119, 1973.

Crisis intervention with victims of rape, by S. S. Fox, et al. SOC WORK 17(1):37-42, January, 1972.

Law enforcement's participation in crisis counseling for rape victims, by J. Stratton. POLICE CHIEF 43(3):46-49, 1976.

Rape and nursing intervention: locating resources, by S. Louie. IMPRINT 22:27+, December, 1975.

Rape and the trauma of inadequate care, by M. S. Welch. PRISM 3:17+, September, 1975.

Rape: breaking the silence; with the rising tide of sexual assaults women have organized crisis centers to assist the victims, by M. Wasserman. PROGRESS 37:19-23, November, 1973.

Rape: hospitals can do more than treat the victim, by H. Frei-lich. HOSP MED STAFF 4:1-7, September, 1975.

Rape: interruption of the therapeutic process by external stress, by A. Werner. PSYCHOTHERAPY: THEORY RES & PRAC 9(4):349-351, Winter, 1972.

VICTIMS—COUNSELING (cont.)

Rape victim counseling: the legal process; adapted from *Rape: Victims of Crisis*, by A. W. Burgess, et al. J NATL ASSN WOMEN DEANS ADM & COUNSEL 38:24-31, Fall, 1974.

Rx for rape the listening ear. EMER MED 7:240-243+, February, 1975.

What to do for victims of rape, by C. R. Hayman, et al. RES STAFF PHYSICIAN 19:29-32, August, 1973.

What to do for victims of rape, by C. R. Hayman, et al. MED TIMES 101:47-51, June, 1973.

When the problem is rape, by B. L. Slaw. RN 35:27-29, April, 1972.

VICTIMS—INTERVIEWING

Guidelines for the interview and examination of alleged rape victims: California Medical Association. WEST J MED 123: 420-422, November, 1975.

VICTIMS—LEGAL RIGHTS

Accountability: a right of the rape victim, by A. W. Burgess, et al. J PSYCHIAT NURSING MENT HEALTH SERV 13:11-16, May-June, 1975.

Accountability and rights of rape victim, by A. W. Burgess, et al. AM J ORTHOP 44(2):182, 1974.

Criminal law—psychiatric examination of prosecutrix in rape case. NC L REV 45:234, December, 1966.

Evidence—admissibility—in a trial for rape, prosecutrix may not be cross examined as to specific acts of prior sexual conduct with men other than defendant, whether the purpose of such cross-examination is to establish her consent as an affirmative defense or to impeach her credibility as a witness. GA L REV 8:973-983, Summer, 1974.

High count backs naming of rape victims in news. ED & PUB 108:11+, March 8, 1975.

In defense of Sis Joanne: for ourselves and history, by M. R. Karenga. BLACK SCHOLAR 6:37-42, July, 1975.

Joanne Little: America goes on trial. FREEDOMWAYS 15(2): 87-88, 1975.

Joanne Little: the dialectics of rape, by A. Davis. MS 3:74-77+, June, 1975.

New rights for rape victims, by A. A. Sant. MAJ REP 4:9, February 8, 1975.

Ohio's new rape law: does it protect complainant at the expense of the rights of the accused? AKRON L REV 9:337-359, Fall, 1975.

Psychiatric and legal aspects of statutory rape, pregnancy and abortion in juveniles, by M. Shopper. J PSYCH & L 1(3): 275-295, Fall, 1973.

Rape in Illinois: a denial of equal protection. JOHN MARSHAL J 8:457-496, Spring, 1975.

Rape: the victim and the criminal justice system, by L. L. Holmstrom, et al. INTERNATL J CRIM & PENOL 3:101-110, May, 1975.

Rape: the victim as defendant, by S. Landau. TRIAL 10:19+, July-August, 1974.

Rape victim: a victim of society and the law. WILLAMETTE L J 11:36-55, Winter, 1974.

The rape victim and due process, by A. Blumberg. CASE AND

VICTIMS—LEGAL RIGHTS (cont.)

COM 80:3-17, November-December, 1975.

Rape victim counseling: the legal process; adapted from *Rape: Victims of Crisis,* by A. W. Burgess, et al. J NATL ASSN WOMEN DEANS ADM & COUNSEL 38:24-31, Fall, 1974.

The rape victim: is she also the unintended victim of the law?, by A. Taylor. N Y TIMES June 15, 1971.

Rape/whom does the law protect, by Mastalli. COLL PRESS SER 45:4, March 20, 1974.

Right to privacy; overturning of a Georgia statute forbidding publication of a rape victim's name, by J. K. Footlick, et al. NEWSWK 85:66, March 17, 1975.

Social, legal, and psychological effects of rape on the victim, by J. J. Peters. PA MED 78(2):34-36, February, 1975.

Special cases: rape victims' plight gets wide attention from police courts, by J. C. Simpson. WALL ST J 186:1+, July 14, 1975.

To be minor and female, by J. Strouse. MS 1:70-75+, August, 1972.

Top goal of women's groups: protecting rape victims rights, by B. Keppel. CAL J 5:222-224, July, 1974.

Twice traumatized: the rape victim and the court, by C. Bohmer, et al. JUDICATURE 58:391-399, March, 1975.

Women/know your rights, by Krista. GREAT SPECKLED BIRD 7(16):4, April 22, 1974.

VICTIMS—MEDICAL ASPECTS

Another look at the care of the rape victim, by J. W. Hanss, Jr. ARIZ MED 32(8):634-635, August, 1975.

Battery and rape; medico-ethical problems in the examination and reporting to the police, by H. T. Cremers. NED TIJD-SCHR GENEESKD 119(32):1259-1262, August 9, 1975.

Biofeedback treatment of a rape-related psychophysiological cardiovascular disorder, by G. G. Abel, et al. PSYCHOS MED 37(1):85, 1975.

Dispute over care of Baltimore County rape victims settled; hospitals to be paid. AM MED NEWS 18:12, August, 1975.

Estrogen therapy after rape?, by B. Paulshock, et al. ANN INTERN MED 72:961, June, 1970.

Examination of semen and saliva in a single stain, by L. O. Barsegiants. SUD MED EKSPERT 14:30-32, October-December, 1971.

Examining the sexual assault victim, by A. F. Schiff. J FL MED ASS 56:731-739, September, 1960.

Guidelines for the interview and examination of alleged rape victims: California Medical Association. WEST J MED 123:420-422, November, 1975.

Gynaecological findings in sexual offenses, by Sklovska. METAL CESK GYNEKOL 40(10):721-723, December, 1975.

Illinois hospitals required to give rape victims free care. HOSP 49:17, September 16, 1975.

Liability to punishment for pregnancy interruptions following rape, in the new penal code? by H. J. Rieger. DEUTSCH MED WSCHR 94:507, March 7, 1969.

Medical aspects of rape, by A. Frank, et al. MADEMOISELLE 82:46-47, February, 1976.

Medical assessment of the sexually assaulted female, by C. A. Ringrose. MED TRIAL TECHN QUART 15:59-61, December, 1968.

Medical care for the sexually assaulted, by J. H. Davis. J FL MED ASS 61:588, July, 1974.

Medical examination in sexual offenses, by D. M. Paul. MED SCI & L 15:154-162, July, 1975.

The medical examination of cases of rape, by W. F. Enos, et al. J FORENSIC SCI 17(1):50-56, January, 1972.

Medical investigation of alleged rape, by I. Root, et al. WEST J MED 120:329-333, April, 1974.

Medico-legal considerations on the presence of a tampax in the vaginal orifice during a rape, by P. L'Epee, et al. MED LEG DOMM CORPOR 1:180-181, April, 1968.

Medicolegal examination of the hymen. Analytical study of 384 medicolegal expertises of sexual assaults, by A. Debarge, et al. MED LEG DOMM CORPOR 6:298-300, July-September, 1973.

Nidation inhibition and abortion following rape, by E. Bohm, et al. MED KLIN 66:989-996, July 2, 1971.

On the use of a particular technic to make more precise diagnosis of hymenal integrity, by G. Dellepiane. MINERVA MEDICOLEG 84:37-43, May-June, 1964.

Postcoital estrogens in cases of rape, by M. G. Chapman. NEW ENG J MED 280:277, January 30, 1969.

A public health program for sexually assaulted females, by C. R. Hayman, et al. PUB HEALTH REP 82:497-504, June, 1967.

Rape and the trauma of inadequate care, by M. S. Welch. PRISM 3:17+, September, 1975.

Rape: hospitals can do more than treat the victim, by H. Frei-
lich. HOSP MED STAFF 4:1-7, September, 1975.

Rape needs a special examination, by A. F. Schiff. EMER MED
3:28-29, October, 1971.

Rape or suspected rape cases. J LOUISIANA MED SOC 119:
319-320, August, 1967.

Rape victim in the emergency ward, by A. W. Burgess, et al.
AM J NURSING 73:1740-1745, October, 1973.

Rape victims—the invisible patients, by V. Price. CAN NURSE
71(4):29-34, April, 1975.

Rape victims: the unpopular patients, by E. LeBourdais. DI-
MEN HEALTH SERV 53:12-14, March, 1976.

Sexual assault program: District of Columbia, by R. L. Standard.
MED ANN DC 41:95-96, February, 1972.

Sexual assault: signs and symptoms, by A. W. Burgess, et al. J
EMERGENCY NURSING   1:10-15, March-April, 1975.

Sexual crimes and the medical examiner: interview with Milton
Helpern. MED ASPECTS OF HUM SEXUAL 8(4):161-168,
April, 1974.

Standard rape investigation form, by W. F. Enos, et al. VA MED
MON 101:43-44, January, 1974.

Suspected rape. MED LEG BULL 209:1-4, September, 1970.

Total health needs of the rape victim, by A. Kaufman, et al.
J FAM PRACT 2(3):225-229, June, 1975.

What to do for victims of rape, by C. R. Hayman, et al. MED
TIMES 101:47-51, June, 1973.

What to do for victims of rape, by C. R. Hayman, et al. RES

VICTIMS—MEDICAL ASPECTS (cont.)

STAFF PHYSICIAN 19:29-32, August, 1973.

When the problem is rape, by B. L. Shaw. RN 35:27-29, April, 1972.

VICTIMS—PSYCHOLOGY

Coping behavior of the rape victim, by A. W. Burgess, et al. AM J PSYCH 133:413-418, April, 1976.

The molested young female. Evaluation and therapy of alleged rape, by J. L. Breen, et al. PEDIATR CLIN NORTH AM 19:717-725, August, 1972.

Patterns of response among victims of rape, by S. Sutherland, et al. AM J ORTHO 40:503-511, April, 1970.

Psychiatric and legal aspects of statutory rape, pregnancy and abortion in juveniles, by M. Shopper. J PSYCH & L 1(3): 275-295, Fall, 1973.

Rape: interruption of the therapeutic process by external stress, by A. Werner. PSYCHOTHERAPY: THEORY RES & PRAC 9(4):349-351, Winter, 1972.

Rape: the ultimate violation of the self, by E. Hilberman. AM J PSYCH 133:436-437, April, 1976.

Rape victim: psychodynamic considerations, by M. T. Notman, et al. AM J PSYCH 133:408-413, April, 1976.

Social, legal, and psychological effects of rape on the victim, by J. J. Peters. PA MED 78(2):34-36, February, 1975.

Worthlessness, disgust, shame: this is the first stage in a woman's reaction to rape, by K. Whitehorn. OBSERVER 17, August 11, 1974.

WOMEN'S ATTITUDES

But what do we do with our rage?, by G. Steinem. MS 3:51, May, 1975.

Female university student and staff perceptions of rape, by M. H. Herman, et al. J NATL ASSN WOMEN DEANS ADM & COUNSEL 38:20-23, Fall, 1974.

Intelligent woman's guide to sex: social rape, by K. Durbin. MADEMOISELLE 81:58, September, 1975.

Is rape what women really want?, by C. Calvert. MADEMOISELLE 78:134-135+, March, 1974.

It is always the woman who is raped, by D. Metzger. AM J PSYCH 133:405-408, April, 1976.

Like Anns gynecologist or time I was almost raped—personal narratives in womens rap groups, by S. Kalcik. J AM FOLKLO 88(347):3-11, 1975.

New York women discuss rape, by Hardy. MILITANT 35(17): 17, May 7, 1971.

Rape: the ultimate violation of the self, by E. Hilberman. AM J PSYCH 133:436-437, April, 1976.

What can you say about laws that tell a man: if you rob a woman, you might as well rape her too?, by M. W. Lear. REDBK 139:83+, September, 1972.

What it means to be raped, by K. Whitehorn. OBSERVER 18, June 1, 1975.

WOMEN'S RESPONSE

How to tell if you're being raped—and what to do about it; excerpt from *The Womansbook*, by V. Billings. REDBK 144:70+, November, 1974.

WOMEN'S RESPONSE (cont.)

New York women discuss rape, by Hardy. MILITANT 35(17): 17, May 7, 1971.

Our sisters speak. Rape: the response. WOMEN: A J OF LIB 3:2.

Rape and what to do about it, by J. Kole. HARP BAZ 109:118-119+, March, 1976.

Rape: breaking the silence; with the rising tide of sexual assaults women have organized crisis centers to assist the victims, by M. Wasserman. PROGRESS 37:19-23, November, 1973.

Rape victims tell libbers what it's like, by M. McNellis. N Y SUNDAY NEWS 36, April 18, 1971.

Top goal of women's groups: protecting rape victims rights, by B. Keepel. CAL J 5:222-224, July, 1974.

What to do about rape in a third world neighborhood: a white woman's self-criticism, by K. Williams. AIN'T I A WOMAN 3:5, July 20, 1973.

What women are doing about the ugliest crime, by A. Lake. GOOD H 179:84-85+, August, 1974.

Why we aren't laughing...any more, by N. Weisstein. MS 2:5, November, 1973.

Women against rape. TIME 101:104, April 23, 1973.

Women hit biased rape laws, by Blakkan. GUARDIAN 26(21): 9, March 6, 1974.

Women hold conference on rape, by Blakkan. GUARDIAN 23(32):6, May 12, 1971.

Women move to stop rape, by Hing. ANN ARBOR SUN 2(6): 10, March 22, 1974.

WOMEN'S RESPONSE (cont.)

Women speak out on rape. WOMEN'S WORLD April 15, 1971.

AUTHOR INDEX

AUTHOR INDEX

AUTHOR INDEX

AUTHOR INDEX

AUTHOR INDEX

AUTHOR INDEX